The Essential Handbook for Writers

Jane E. Aaron

also published under the title
The Little, Brown Essential Handbook for Writers

HarperPerennial
A Division of HarperCollins*Publishers*

HarperCollins books may be purchased for educational, business, or sales promotional use. For information, please write: Special Markets Department, HarperCollins Publishers, Inc., 10 East 53rd Street, New York, N.Y. 10022.

FIRST HARPERPERENNIAL EDITION

ISBN 0-06-273296-X

CONTENTS

Note: *The symbol* ESL *indicates material especially for writers using English as a second language.*

USING THIS BOOK

This little book contains essential information for writers in and out of school. Clarity and style, grammar, punctuation, mechanics, source documentation, usage—all the basics appear in a convenient, accessible format. (To see how the book works, look at the visual guide inside the back cover.) Explanations consider writers who are unfamiliar with the terminology of writing: needless terms are omitted, and essential terms, marked °, are defined in the Glossary of Terms. Material especially for writers using English as a second language is marked ESL. Examples come from a wide range of subjects, science to literature to business.

To get the most from a little book like this, you need to use it in a larger context. That's why the first thing you see inside the front cover is a Writer's Checklist covering the entire process of writing. Contrary to much popular opinion, writing is *not* solely, or even primarily, a matter of correctness. True, any written message will find a more receptive audience if it is correct in grammar, punctuation, and similar matters. But these should come late in the process, after you've allowed yourself to discover what you want to say and how you want to say it, freeing yourself to make mistakes along the way. As one writer put it, you need to get the clay on the potter's wheel before you can shape it into a bowl, and you need to shape the bowl before you can perfect it. So get your clay on the wheel and work with it until it looks like a bowl. Then consult this book.

Acknowledgments

A number of teachers helped me shape and edit this book. Many thanks to Larry Beason, Eastern Washington University; C. Jerome Binus, Butler County Community College; Darlynn R. Fink, Clarion University of Pennsylvania; Kim Flachmann, California State University, Bakersfield; Ted E. Johnston, El Paso Community College; Nancy Joseph, York College of Pennsylvania; Martha Kearns, University of Nevada, Reno; John Osborne, Butte College; Elizabeth Renfro, California State University, Chico; and Richard Sax, Madonna University.

Thanks also to Andrew Christensen and to my friends at HarperCollins, especially Patricia Rossi, Mark Scott, Ann Stypuloski, Steven Pisano, and Dorothy Bungert.

I

CLARITY AND STYLE

1
COORDINATION AND SUBORDINATION

Coordination and subordination make it possible to connect and stress ideas within sentences.

Coordination for readability

Use COORDINATION to show that two or more elements in a sentence are equally important in meaning.

- Link two completed sentences (main clauses°) with a comma and a coordinating conjunction° (*and, but, or, nor, for, so, yet*).

  Independence Hall in Philadelphia is now restored, but *fifty years ago it was in bad shape.*

- Link two main clauses with a semicolon alone or a semicolon and a conjunctive adverb,° such as *however, indeed,* or *therefore.*

  The building was standing; however, *it suffered from decay and vandalism.*

- Within clauses, link words and word groups with a coordinating conjunction (*and, but, or, nor*).

  The people and officials of the nation were indifferent to Independence Hall or *took it for granted.*

Coordination both clarifies meaning and smooths choppy sentences.

CHOPPY SENTENCES	We should not rely so heavily on oil. Coal and uranium are also overused. We have a substantial energy resource in the moving waters of our rivers. Smaller streams add to the total volume of water. The resource renews itself. Coal and oil are irreplaceable. Uranium is also irreplaceable. The cost of water does not increase much over time. The costs of coal, oil, and uranium rise dramatically.

° The degree sign (°) marks every term defined in the Glossary of Terms, beginning on page 126.

IDEAS
COORDINATED
We should not rely so heavily on coal, oil, and uranium, for we have a substantial energy resource in the moving waters of our rivers and streams. Coal, oil, and uranium are irreplaceable and thus subject to dramatic cost increases; water, however, is self-renewing and more stable in cost.

NOTE: A string of main clauses connected by *and* implies that all ideas are equally important and creates a dull, plodding rhythm. Use subordination (see below) to revise such excessive coordination.

Subordination for emphasis

Use SUBORDINATION to indicate that some elements in a sentence are less important than others for your meaning. Usually, the main idea appears in the main clause,° and supporting information appears in subordinate structures such as the following:

• Subordinate clauses° beginning with *although, because, if, who (whom), that, which,* or another subordinating word.

Although production costs have declined, they are still high.
Costs, *which include labor and facilities,* are difficult to control.

• Phrases.°

Despite some decline, production costs are still high.
Costs, *including labor and facilities,* are difficult to control.

• Single words.

Declining costs have not matched prices.
Labor costs are difficult to control.

Subordination can transform a monotonous string of main clauses into a more emphatic and interesting passage.

STRING OF MAIN
CLAUSES
In recent years computer prices have dropped, and production costs have dropped more slowly, and computer manufacturers have had to struggle, for their profits have been shrinking.

REVISED
Because production costs have dropped more slowly *than computer prices* in recent years, computer manufacturers have had to struggle *with shrinking profits.*

Generally, subordinate clauses give the most emphasis to secondary information, phrases give less, and single words give the least.

2
PARALLELISM

PARALLELISM is a similarity of grammatical form between two or more coordinated elements.

The air is dirtied by	factories	belching	smoke
and	cars	spewing	exhaust.

With parallelism, form reflects meaning: the parts of compound constructions have the same function and importance, so they also have the same grammatical form.

Parallelism with *and, but, or, nor, yet*

The coordinating conjunctions° signal a need for parallelism.

The industrial base is *shifting* and *shrinking.*

Politicians seldom *acknowledge the problem* or *propose alternatives.*

Industrial workers are understandably disturbed *that they are losing their jobs* and *that no one seems to care.*

FAULTY   Three reasons why steel companies keep losing money are that their plants are inefficient, high labor costs, and foreign competition is increasing.

REVISED   Three reasons why steel companies keep losing money are *inefficient plants, high labor costs,* and *increasing foreign competition.*

NOTE: Be careful not to omit needed words in parallel structures.

FAULTY   Many workers find it difficult to have faith and work for the future.

REVISED   Many workers find it difficult to have faith *in* and work for the future. [*Faith* and *work* require different prepositions,° so both must be stated.]

Parallellism with *both . . . and, either . . . or,* etc.

Correlative conjunctions° stress equality and balance between elements. Parallelism confirms the equality.

At the end of the novel, Huck Finn both *rejects society's values by turning down money and a home* and *affirms his own values by setting out for "the territory."*

With correlative conjunctions, the element after the second connector must match the element after the first connector.

FAULTY   Huck Finn learns <u>not only</u> that human beings have an enormous capacity for folly <u>but also</u> enormous dignity. [The first element includes *that human beings have;* the second element does not.]

REVISED   Huck Finn learns *that human beings have not only* an enormous capacity for folly but also enormous dignity. [Repositioning *not only* makes the two elements parallel.]

3
VARIETY AND DETAILS

Writing that's interesting as well as clear has varied sentences that are well textured with details.

Varied sentence lengths and structures

In most contemporary writing, sentences tend to vary from about ten to about forty words, with an average of fifteen to twenty-five words. If your sentences are all at one extreme or the other, your readers may have difficulty focusing on main ideas and seeing the relations among them.

• If most of your sentences contain thirty-five words or more, you probably need to break some up into shorter, simpler sentences.

• If most of your sentences contain fewer than ten or fifteen words, you probably need to add details to them (p. 7) or combine them through coordination (p. 2) and subordination (p. 3).

6 · Variety and details

3

A good way to hold readers' attention is to vary the structure of sentences so that they do not all follow the same pattern, like soldiers in a parade. Some suggestions:

• Enliven strings of main clauses° by subordinating the less important information.

MONOTONOUS   The moon is now drifting away from the earth. It moves away at the rate of about one inch a year. Our days on earth are getting longer, and they grow a thousandth of a second longer every century. A month will someday be forty-seven of our present days long, and we might eventually lose the moon altogether. Such great planetary movement rightly concerns astronomers, but it need not worry us. It will take 50 million years.

REVISED   The moon is now drifting away from the earth *at the rate of about one inch a year. At the rate of a thousandth of a second or so every century,* our days on earth are getting longer. A month will someday be forty-seven of our present days long, *if we don't eventually lose the moon altogether.* Such great planetary movement rightly concerns astronomers, but it need not worry us. It will take 50 million years.

• Vary the beginnings of sentences so that some do not begin with their subjects.°

MONOTONOUS   The lawyer cross-examined the witness for two days. The witness had expected to be dismissed within an hour and was visibly irritated. He did not cooperate. He was reprimanded by the judge.

REVISED   *For two days,* the lawyer cross-examined the witness. *Expecting to be dismissed within an hour,* the witness was visibly irritated. He did not cooperate. *Indeed,* he was reprimanded by the judge.

• Occasionally, to achieve special emphasis, reverse the usual word order of a sentence.

A dozen witnesses testified, and the defense attorney barely questioned eleven of them. *The twelfth, however, he grilled.* [Compare normal word order: *He grilled the twelfth, however.*]

Details

Relevant details such as facts and examples create the texture and life that keep readers awake and help them grasp your meaning. For instance:

FLAT   Constructed after World War II, Levittown, NY, consisted of thousands of houses in two basic styles. Over the decades, residents have altered the houses so dramatically that the original styles are often unrecognizable.

DETAILED   Constructed *on potato fields* after World War II, Levittown, NY, consisted of *more than 17,000* houses in *Cape Cod and ranch* styles. Over the decades, residents have *added expansive front porches, punched dormer windows through roofs, converted garages to sun porches, and otherwise* altered the houses so dramatically that the original styles are often unrecognizable.

4

APPROPRIATE WORDS

A country as diverse as the United States naturally encompasses varied subcultures with their own rich and vital vocabularies, such as the dialects of many African-Americans and Hawaiians or the technical slang of computer hackers. The common language that brings all speakers together is standard English, usually defined as the English expected and used by educated readers and writers. In situations calling for standard English, including most academic and business writing, some specialized vocabularies should be used only cautiously, as when aiming for a particular effect with an audience you know will appreciate it. Other vocabularies, especially those expressing prejudice, should be avoided altogether.

Slang

SLANG is the insider language used by a group, such as musicians or football players, to reflect common experiences and to make technical references efficient. The following example is from an essay on the slang of "skaters" (skateboarders):

> Curtis slashed ultra-punk crunchers on his longboard, while the Rube-man flailed his usual Gumbyness on tweaked frontsides and lofty fakie ollies.
> —MILES ORKIN, "Mucho Slingage by the Pool"

Though valuable within a group, slang is often too private or imprecise for academic or business writing.

Colloquial language

COLLOQUIAL LANGUAGE is the everyday spoken language, including expressions such as *get together, go crazy,* and *do the dirty work.* It is labeled "informal" or "colloquial" in your dictionary.

Colloquial language suits informal writing, and an occasional colloquial word can help you achieve a desired emphasis in otherwise formal writing. But most colloquial language is not precise enough for academic or career writing.

Nonstandard language

Some dialects of English, spoken by many intelligent people, use expressions that may be considered wrong by readers who do not know the dialects. These expressions are not included in standard English and are labeled "nonstandard" in dictionaries. Examples are *nowheres, hisn, hern, hisself, theirselves, them dishes, this here, that there, knowed, throwed, hadn't ought, could of, didn't never, haven't no, might could.* Unless you have a good reason for using nonstandard expressions, avoid them in speaking and writing situations calling for standard English.

Technical words

All disciplines and professions rely on specialized language that allows the members to communicate precisely and efficiently with each other. Chemists, for instance, have their *phosphatides,* and literary critics have their *subtexts.* When writing to a nonspecialist audience, avoid unnecessary technical terms and carefully define necessary terms.

Indirect and pretentious writing

Small, plain, and direct words are usually preferable to big, showy, or evasive words. Take special care to avoid the following:

- EUPHEMISMS are presumably inoffensive words that substitute for words deemed potentially offensive or too blunt, such as *passed away* for *died* or *misspeak* for *lie*. Use euphemisms only when you know that blunt, truthful words would needlessly hurt or offend members of your audience.
- DOUBLE TALK (also called DOUBLESPEAK or WEASEL WORDS) is language intended to confuse or to be misunderstood: the *revenue enhancement* that is really a tax, the *biodegradable* bags that last decades. Double talk has no place in honest writing.
- PRETENTIOUS WRITING is fancy language that is more elaborate than its subject requires. Choose your words for their exactness and economy. The big, ornate word may be tempting, but pass it up. Your readers will be grateful.

PRETENTIOUS	Many institutions of higher education recognize the need for youth at the threshold of maturity to confront the choice of life's endeavor and thus require students to select a field of concentration.
REVISED	Many colleges and universities force students to make decisions about their careers by requiring them to select a major.

Sexist and other biased language

Language can reflect and perpetuate inaccurate and hurtful prejudices toward groups of people, especially racial, ethnic, religious, age, and sexual groups. Insulting language reflects more poorly on the user than on the person or persons designated. Unbiased language does not submit to stereotypes. It refers to people as they would wish to be referred to.

Among the most subtle and persistent biased language is sexist language that distinguishes needlessly between men and women in such matters as occupation, ability, behavior, temperament, and maturity. The following guidelines can help you eliminate sexist language from your writing:

• Avoid demeaning and patronizing language.

SEXIST   Ladies are entering almost every occupation.

REVISED   *Women* are entering almost every occupation.

SEXIST   President Reagan came to Nancy's defense.

REVISED   President Reagan came to *Mrs. Reagan's* defense.

• Avoid occupational or social stereotypes.

SEXIST   The caring doctor commends his nurse when she does a good job.

REVISED   Caring *doctors* commend *their nurses* on jobs well done.

• Avoid using *man* or words containing *man* to refer to all human beings.

SEXIST   Man has not reached the limits of social justice.

REVISED   *Humankind* (or *Humanity*) has not reached the limits of social justice.

SEXIST   The furniture consists of manmade materials.

REVISED   The furniture consists of *synthetic* materials.

• Avoid using *he* to refer to both genders. (See also p. 35.)

SEXIST   The person who studies history knows his roots.

REVISED   The person who studies history knows *his* or *her* roots.

REVISED   *People* who study history know *their* roots.

5

EXACT WORDS

To write clearly and effectively, you will want to find the words that fit your meaning exactly and convey your attitude precisely.

The right word for your meaning

If readers are to understand you, you must use words according to their established meanings.

• Become acquainted with a dictionary. Consult it whenever you are unsure of a word's meaning.

• Distinguish between similar-sounding words that have widely different meanings.

INEXACT   Older people often suffer *infirmaries* [places for the sick].

EXACT   Older people often suffer *infirmities* [disabilities].

Some words, called HOMONYMS, sound exactly alike but differ in meaning: for example, *principal/principle* or *rain/reign/rein*. (Many homonyms and near-homonyms are listed in the Glossary of Usage, p. 114.)

• Distinguish between words with related but distinct meanings.

INEXACT   Television commercials *continuously* [unceasingly] interrupt programming.

EXACT   Television commercials *continually* [regularly] interrupt programming.

• Distinguish between words that have similar basic meanings but different emotional associations, or CONNOTATIONS.

It is a *daring* plan. [The plan is bold and courageous.]
It is a *reckless* plan. [The plan is thoughtless and risky.]

Many dictionaries list and distinguish such SYNONYMS, words with approximately, but often not exactly, the same meanings.

Concrete and specific words

Clear, exact writing balances abstract and general words, which outline ideas and objects, with concrete and specific words, which sharpen and solidify.

• ABSTRACT WORDS name qualities and ideas: *beauty, inflation, management, culture, liberal.* CONCRETE WORDS name things we can know by our five senses of sight, hearing, touch, taste, and smell: *sleek, humming, brick, bitter, musty.*
• GENERAL WORDS name classes or groups of things, such as *buildings, weather,* or *birds,* and include all the varieties of the class. SPECIFIC WORDS limit a general class, such as *buildings,* by naming one of its varieties, such as *skyscraper, Victorian courthouse,* or *hut.*

Abstract and general statements need development with concrete and specific details. For example:

| VAGUE | The size of his hands made his smallness real. [How big were his hands? How small was he?] |
| EXACT | Not until I saw his white, doll-like hands did I realize that he stood a full head shorter than most other men. |

Idioms

IDIOMS are expressions in any language that do not fit the rules for meaning or grammar—for instance, *put up with, plug away at, make off with.*

Because they are not governed by rules, idioms usually cause particular difficulty for people learning to speak and write a new language. But even native speakers of English misuse some idioms involving prepositions,° such as *agree on a plan, agree to a proposal,* and *agree with a person* or *charge for a purchase* and *charge with a crime.*

When in doubt about an idiom, consult your dictionary under the main word (*agree* and *charge* in the examples). (See also pp. 29–30 on verbs with particles.)

Trite expressions

TRITE EXPRESSIONS, or CLICHÉS, are phrases so old and so often repeated that they become stale. Examples include *better late than never, beyond the shadow of a doubt, face the music, green with envy, ladder of success, point with pride, sneaking suspicion,* and *wise as an owl.*

To prevent clichés from sliding into your writing, be wary of any expression you have heard or used before. Substitute fresh words of your own, or restate the idea in plain language.

6
CONCISENESS

Concise writing makes every word count. Conciseness is not the same as mere brevity: detail and originality should not be cut with needless words. Rather, the length of an expression should be appropriate to the thought.

You may find yourself writing wordily when you are unsure of your subject or when your thoughts are tangled. It's fine, even necessary, to stumble and grope while drafting. But you should straighten out your ideas and eliminate wordiness during revision and editing.

Empty words and phrases

Cutting or reducing empty words and phrases will make your writing move faster and work harder.

WORDY   As far as I am concerned, because of the fact that a situation of discrimination continues to exist in the field of medicine, women have not at the present time achieved equality with men.

CONCISE   Because of continuing discrimination in medicine, women have not yet achieved equality with men.

Some empty expressions can be cut entirely, such as *all things considered, as far as I'm concerned, for all intents and purposes, in a manner of speaking,* and *more or less.* Others can also be cut, usually along with some of the words around them: *area, aspect, case, element, factor, field, kind, manner, nature, situation, thing, type.* Still others can be reduced from several words to a single word—for instance, *at the present time* and *in today's society* both reduce to *now.*

Unneeded repetition

Unnecessary repetition weakens sentences.

WORDY   Many unskilled workers *without training in a particular job* are unemployed *and do not have any work.*

CONCISE   Many unskilled workers are unemployed.

Be especially alert to phrases that say the same thing twice. In the following examples, only the underlined words are needed: *circle around, consensus of opinion, cooperate together, final completion, the future to come, important (basic) essentials, repeat again, return again, square (round) in shape, surrounding circumstances.*

Sentence combining

Often the information in two or more sentences can be combined into one tight sentence.

WORDY   The French and British collaborated on building the Channel Tunnel. The tunnel links France and Britain. The French drilled from Sangatte. The British drilled from Dover.

CONCISE   The French and British collaborated on building the Channel Tunnel between their countries, the French drilling from Sangatte and the British from Dover.

Reduced clauses and phrases

Modifiers° can be expanded or contracted depending on the emphasis you want to achieve. (Generally, the longer a construction, the more emphasis it has.) When editing your sentences, consider whether any modifiers can be reduced without loss of emphasis or clarity.

WORDY   The tunnel, *which was drilled for twenty-three miles,* runs *through a bed of solid chalk that lies under the English Channel.*

CONCISE   The *twenty-three-mile* tunnel runs *through solid chalk under the English Channel.*

Strong verbs

Weak verbs such as *is, has,* and *make* stall sentences and usually carry the extra baggage of unneeded or vague words.

WORDY   The drillers *made slow advancement,* and costs *were over* $5 million a day. The slow progress *was worrisome for* backers, who *had had expectations of* high profits.

CONCISE   The drillers *advanced slowly,* and costs *topped* $5 million a day. The slow progress *worried* backers, who *had expected* high profits.

Active voice

A verb's active voice° uses fewer words than the passive voice° and is much more direct because it names the performer of the verb's action up front. Reserve the passive voice mainly for emphasizing the receiver rather than the performer of the verb's action. Otherwise, prefer the active voice.

WORDY PASSIVE   As many as *fifteen feet* of chalk an hour *could be chewed through* by the drill.

CONCISE ACTIVE   The *drill could chew through* as many as fifteen feet of chalk an hour.

Unneeded *there is* or *it is*

Sentences beginning *there is* or *it is* (called expletive con-
structions°) are sometimes useful to emphasize a change in
direction, but usually they just add needless words.

WORDY   *There are more than half a million shareholders who*
        have invested in the tunnel. *It is they and the banks
        that* expect to profit when the tunnel opens to trains.

CONCISE *More than half a million shareholders* have invested
         in the tunnel. *They and the banks* expect to profit
         when the tunnel opens to trains.

6

II

SENTENCE PARTS AND PATTERNS

7

VERB FORMS

Verb forms may give you trouble when the verb is irregular, when you omit certain endings, or when you need to use helping verbs.

Sing/sang/sung and other irregular verbs

About 200 IRREGULAR VERBS in English create their past-tense form° and past participle° in some way besides adding *-d* or *-ed*, as in *I walk. Yesterday I walked. In the past I have walked.* Irregular verbs include *become* (*became/become*), *begin* (*began/begun*), *give* (*gave/given*), and *sing* (*sang/sung*): *I sing. Yesterday I sang. In the past I have sung.*

Check a dictionary under a verb's plain form° if you have any doubt about the verb's other forms. If the verb is regular, the dictionary will follow the plain form with the *-d* or *-ed* form. If the verb is irregular, the dictionary will follow the plain form with the past-tense form and then the past participle. If the dictionary gives only one irregular form after the plain form, the past-tense form and past participle are the same (*think, thought, thought*).

-s and *-ed* verb endings

Speakers of some English dialects and some other languages omit verb endings that are required by standard English. One is the *-s* ending on the verb when the subject° is *he, she, it,* or a singular noun° and the verb's action occurs in the present.

The roof *leaks* (not *leak*).	Tina *has* (not *have*) a car.
He *doesn't* (not *don't*) care.	She *is* (not *be*) happy.

Another verb ending required by standard English is the *-ed* or *-d* ending when (1) the verb's action occurred in the past, (2) the verb form functions as a modifier,° or (3) the verb form combines with a form of *be* or *have*.

I *used* (not *use*) to dance.
He was *supposed* (not *suppose*) to call.

We *bagged* (not *bag*) groceries yesterday.
Sue has *asked* (not *ask*) us.

Helping verbs + main verbs ESL

Helping verbs° combine with main verbs° in specific ways.

Form of *be* + present participle

Create the progressive tenses° with *be, am, is, are, was, were,* or *been* followed by the main verb's present participle.°

She *is working* on a new book.

Be and *been* require additional helping verbs to form progressive tenses.

can	might	should			have	
could	must	will	*be* working		has	*been* working
may	shall	would			had	

When forming the progressive tenses, be sure to use the -*ing* form of the main verb.

NOTE: Verbs that express mental states or activities rather than physical actions do not usually appear in the progressive tenses. These verbs include *adore, appear, believe, belong, have, hear, know, like, love, need, see, taste, think, understand,* and *want.*

FAULTY She *is wanting* to understand contemporary ethics.

REVISED She *wants* to understand contemporary ethics.

Form of *be* + past participle

Create the passive voice° with *be, am, is, are, was, were, being,* or *been* followed by the main verb's past participle.°

Her latest book *was completed* in four months.

Be, being, and *been* require additional helping verbs to form the passive voice.

have		am	was	
has	*been* completed	is	were	*being* completed
had		are		

will *be* completed

Be sure to use the main verb's past participle for the passive voice.

NOTE: Use only transitive verbs° to form the passive voice.

FAULTY A philosophy conference *will be occurred* in the same week. [*Occur* is not a transitive verb.]

REVISED A philosophy conference *will occur* in the same week.

Form of *have* + past participle

Four forms of *have* serve as helping verbs: *have, has, had, having.* One of these forms plus the main verb's past participle creates one of the perfect tenses.°

Some students *have complained* about the laboratory.
Others *had complained* before.

Will and other helping verbs sometimes accompany forms of *have* in the perfect tenses.

Several more students *will have complained* by the end of the week.

Form of *do* + plain form

Always with the plain form° of the main verb, three forms of *do* serve as helping verbs: *do, does, did.* These forms have three uses:

- To pose a question: *Whom did the officers arrest?*
- To emphasize the main verb: *They did arrest someone.*
- To negate the main verb, along with *not* or *never: The suspect did not escape.*

Be sure to use the main verb's plain form with any form of *do.*

FAULTY They did *captured* someone.

REVISED They did *capture* someone.

Modal + plain form

The MODALS are ten helping verbs that never change form.

can	may	must	shall	will
could	might	ought	should	would

The modals indicate necessity, obligation, permission, possibility, and other meanings. They are always used with the plain form of the main verb.

They *can speak* English. They *could translate. Will* you *ask* them?

8

VERB TENSES

Definitions and examples of the verb tenses appear on pages 136–37. The following are the most common trouble spots.

Uses of the present tense (*sing*)

The present tense° has several uses.

Action occurring now
She *understands* what you mean.

Habitual or recurring action
The store *opens* at ten o'clock.

A general truth
The earth *is* round.

Discussion of literature, film, and so on
Huckleberry Finn *has* adventures we all envy.

Future time
The theater *closes* in a month.

Uses of the perfect tenses (*have/had/will have sung*)

The perfect tenses° generally indicate an action completed before another specific time or action. The present perfect tense° also indicates action begun in the past and continued into the present.

Present perfect
The dancer *has visited* here regularly.
He *has performed* here only once.

Past perfect
The dancer *had trained* in Asia before his performance here ten years ago.

Future perfect
He *will have performed* here again by the time this article is published.

Consistency in tense

Within a sentence, the tenses of verbs and verb forms need not be identical as long as they reflect actual changes in time: *Ramon will graduate from college twenty years after his father arrived in America.* But needless shifts in tense will confuse or distract readers.

INCONSISTENT Immediately after Booth *shot* Lincoln, Major Rathbone *threw* himself upon the assassin. But Booth *pulls* a knife and *plunges* it into the major's arm.

REVISED Immediately after Booth *shot* Lincoln, Major Rathbone *threw* himself upon the assassin. But Booth *pulled* a knife and *plunged* it into the major's arm.

Sequence of tenses ESL

The SEQUENCE OF TENSES is the relation between the verb tense in a main clause° and the verb tense in a subordinate clause.° The tenses are often different, as in *He will leave before I arrive.*

Past or past perfect tense in main clause
When the verb in the main clause is in the past tense° or past perfect tense,° the verb in the subordinate clause must also be past or past perfect.

The reseachers *discovered* that people *varied* widely in their knowledge of public events.

The variation *occurred* because respondents *had been born* in different decades.

None of them *had been born* when Warren G. Harding *was* President.

EXCEPTION: Always use the present tense° for a general truth, such as *The earth is round.*

Few *understood* that popular Presidents *are* not necessarily good Presidents.

Conditional sentences
A CONDITIONAL SENTENCE usually consists of a subordinate clause beginning *if, when,* or *unless* and a main clause stating

22 . Verb tenses

the result. The three kinds of conditional sentences use distinctive verbs.

- For factual statements that something always or usually happens whenever something else happens, use the present tense in both clauses.

When a voter *casts* [present] a ballot, he or she *has* [present] complete privacy.

If the linked events occurred in the past, use the past tense in both clauses.

When voters *registered* [past] in some states, they *had* [past] to pay a poll tax.

- For predictions, generally use the present tense in the subordinate clause and the future tense° in the main clause.

Unless citizens *regain* [present] faith in politics, they *will* [future] not *vote*.

Sometimes the verb in the main clause consists of *may, can, should,* or *might* plus the verb's plain form:° *If citizens regain faith, they may vote.*

- For speculations about events that are possible though unlikely, use the past tense in the subordinate clause and *would, could,* or *might* plus the verb's plain form in the main clause.

If voters *had* [past] more confidence, they *would vote* [would + verb] more often.

Use *were* instead of *was* when the subject is *I, he, she, it,* or a singular noun.

If the voter *were* [past] more confident, he or she *would vote* [would + verb] more often.

For events that are impossible now—that are contrary to fact—use the same forms as above (including the distinctive *were* when applicable).

If Lincoln *were* [past] alive, he *might inspire* [might + verb] confidence.

For events that were impossible in the past, use the past perfect tense in the subordinate clause and *would, could,* or *might* plus the present perfect tense° in the main clause.

past perfect   might + present perfect
If Lincoln *had survived* the Civil War, he *might have stabilized* the country.

The last four examples above illustrate the subjunctive mood of verbs. See below.

9
VERB MOOD

The mood° of a verb indicates whether a sentence is a statement or a question (*The theater needs help. Can you help the theater?*), a command (*Help the theater*), or a suggestion, desire, or other nonfactual expression (*I wish I were an actor*).

Consistency in mood

Shifts in mood within a sentence or among related sentences can be confusing. Such shifts occur most frequently in directions.

INCONSISTENT   *Cook* the mixture slowly, and *you should stir* it until the sugar is dissolved.

REVISED   *Cook* the mixture slowly, and *stir* it until the sugar is dissolved.

Subjunctive mood: *I wish I were*

The SUBJUNCTIVE MOOD expresses a suggestion, requirement, or desire, or it states a condition that is contrary to fact (that is, imaginary or hypothetical).

• Suggestion or requirement with the verb *ask, insist, urge, require, recommend,* or *suggest:* use the verb's plain form° with all subjects.

Rules require that every donation *be* mailed.

• Desire or present condition contrary to fact: use the verb's past-tense form;° for *be,* use the past-tense form *were.*

If the theater *were* in better shape and *had* more money, its future would be guaranteed.

• Past condition contrary to fact: use the verb's past-perfect form° (*had* + past participle).

The theater would be better funded if it *had been* better managed.

NOTE: In a sentence expressing a condition contrary to fact, the helping verb° *would* or *could* does not appear in the clause beginning *if.*

NOT   Many people would have helped if they *would have* known.

BUT   Many people would have helped if they *had* known.

10
VERB VOICE

The voice° of a verb tells whether the subject° of the sentence performs the action (active voice°) or is acted upon (passive voice°).

Consistency in voice

A shift in voice (and subject) from one sentence to another can be awkward or even confusing.

INCONSISTENT   In the morning the *children rode* their bicycles; in the afternoon *their skateboards were given* a good workout.

REVISED   In the morning the *children rode* their bicycles; in the afternoon *they gave* their skateboards a good workout.

Active voice vs. passive voice

The active voice is usually stronger, clearer, and more forthright than the passive voice.

WEAK PASSIVE   The exam was thought by us to be unfair because we were tested on material that was not covered in the course.

STRONG ACTIVE   We thought the exam unfair because it tested us on material the course did not cover.

The passive voice is useful in two situations: when the actor is unknown and when the actor is unimportant or less important than the object of the action.

Ray Appleton *was murdered* after he returned home. [The murderer may be unknown, and in any event Ray Appleton's death is the point of the sentence.]

In the first experiment acid *was added* to the solution. [The person who added the acid, perhaps the writer, is less important than the fact that acid was added. Passive sentences are common in scientific writing.]

11

11

AGREEMENT OF SUBJECT AND VERB

A subject° and its verb° should agree in number° and person.°

More *Japanese-Americans live* in Hawaii and California than elsewhere.   subject   verb

Daniel Inouye was the first Japanese-American in Congress.
subject   verb

Words between subject and verb

A catalog of courses and requirements often *baffles* (not *baffle*) students.

The requirements stated in the catalog *are* (not *is*) unclear.

Phrases beginning with *as well as, together with, along with,* and *in addition to* do not change the number of the subject.

The president, as well as the deans, *has* (not *have*) agreed to revise the catalog.

Subjects with *and*

Frost and Roethke *were* American poets who died in the same year.

NOTE: When *each* or *every* precedes the compound subject, the verb is usually singular.

Each man, woman, and child *has* a right to be heard.

Subjects with *or* or *nor*

When parts of a subject are joined by *or* or *nor,* the verb agrees with the nearer part.

Either the painter or the carpenter *knows* the cost.

The cabinets or the bookcases *are* too costly.

When one part of the subject is singular and the other is plural, the sentence will be awkward unless you put the plural part second.

AWKWARD Neither the owners nor the contractor *agrees*.

IMPROVED Neither the contractor nor the owners *agree*.

Everyone and other indefinite pronouns

Indefinite pronouns° such as *everyone, no one,* and *somebody* are usually singular in meaning, and they take singular verbs.

Something *smells*.   Neither *is* right.

A few indefinite pronouns such as *all, any, none,* and *some* may take a singular or plural verb depending on meaning.

All of the money *is* reserved for emergencies.

All of the funds *are* reserved for emergencies.

Team and other collective nouns

A collective noun° such as *team* or *family* takes a singular verb when the group acts as a unit.

The group *agrees* that action is necessary.

But when the group's members act separately, use a plural verb.

The old group *have* gone their separate ways.

Who, which, and *that*

When used as subjects, *who, which,* and *that* refer to another word in the sentence. The verb agrees with this other word.

Mayor Garber ought to listen to the people who *work* for her.

Bardini is the only aide who *has* her ear.

Bardini is one of the aides who *work* unpaid. [Of the aides who work unpaid, Bardini is one.]

Bardini is the only one of the aides who *knows* the community. [Of the aides, only one, Bardini, knows the community.]

News and other singular nouns ending in *-s*

Singular nouns° ending in *-s* include *athletics, economics, mathematics, news, physics, politics,* and *statistics.*

After so long a wait, the news *has* to be good.

Statistics *is* required of psychology majors.

These words take plural verbs when they describe individual items rather than whole bodies of activity or knowledge.

The statistics *prove* him wrong.

Inverted word order

Is voting a right or a privilege?

Are a right and a privilege the same thing?

There *are* differences between them.

Is, are, and other linking verbs

Make a linking verb° agree with its subject, usually the first element in the sentence, not with other words referring to the subject.

Henry's sole support *is* his mother and father.

Henry's mother and father *are* his sole support.

12

OTHER COMPLICATIONS
WITH VERBS ESL

Verbs often combine with other words in idioms° that must be memorized.

Verb + gerund or infinitive

Gerunds° and infinitives° may follow certain verbs but not others. And sometimes the use of a gerund or infinitive with the same verb changes the meaning of the verb.

Either gerund or infinitive

A gerund or an infinitive may follow these verbs with no significant difference in meaning: *begin, continue, hate, like, love, start.*

The pump began *working.* The pump began *to work.*

Meaning change with gerund or infinitive

With four verbs, a gerund has quite a different meaning from an infinitive: *forget, remember, stop, try.*

The engineer stopped *eating.* [He no longer ate.]
The engineer stopped *to eat.* [He stopped in order to eat.]

Gerund, not infinitive

Do not use an infinitive after these verbs: *adore, admit, appreciate, avoid, deny, detest, discuss, enjoy, escape, finish, imagine, miss, practice, put off, quit, recall, resist, risk, suggest, tolerate.*

FAULTY   He finished *to eat* lunch.

REVISED   He finished *eating* lunch.

Infinitive, not gerund

Do not use a gerund after these verbs: *agree, ask, assent, beg, claim, decide, expect, have, hope, manage, mean, offer, plan, pretend, promise, refuse, say, wait, want, wish.*

FAULTY   He decided *checking* the pump.

REVISED   He decided *to check* the pump.

Noun or pronoun + infinitive

Some verbs may be followed by an infinitive alone or by a noun° or pronoun° and an infinitive: *ask, expect, need, want, would like.* A noun or pronoun changes the meaning.

He expected *to watch.*
He expected *his workers to watch.*

Some verbs *must* be followed by a noun or pronoun before an infinitive: *advise, admonish, allow, cause, command, convince, encourage, instruct, order, persuade, remind, require, tell, warn.*

He instructed *his workers to watch.*

Do not use *to* before the infinitive when it follows one of these verbs and a noun or pronoun: *feel, have, hear, let, make* ("force"), *see, watch.*

He let his workers *learn* by observation.

Verb + particle

Some verbs consist of two words: the verb itself and a PARTICLE, a preposition° or adverb° that affects the meaning of the verb. For example: *Look up the answer* (research the answer); *Look over the answer* (check the answer). Many of these two-word verbs are defined in dictionaries. (There are some three-word verbs, too, such as *put up with* and *run out of.*)

Some two-word verbs may be separated in a sentence; others may not.

Inseparable two-word verbs

Verbs and particles that may not be separated by any other words include the following: *catch on, get along, give in, go out, grow up, keep on, look into, run into, run out of, speak up, stay away, take care of.*

FAULTY   Children *grow* quickly *up.*

REVISED   Children *grow up* quickly.

Separable two-word verbs

Most two-word verbs that take direct objects° may be separated by the object.

Parents *help out* their children.
Parents *help* their children *out.*

If the direct object is a pronoun,° the pronoun *must* separate the verb from the particle.

> FAULTY   Parents *help out* them.

> REVISED   Parents *help* them *out*.

The separable two-word verbs include the following: *call off, call up, fill out, fill up, give away, give back, hand in, help out, look over, look up, pick up, point out, put away, put back, put off, take out, take over, try on, try out, turn down.*

PRONOUNS

13

PRONOUN CASE

CASE is the form of a noun° or pronoun° that shows the reader how it functions in a sentence. Definitions and forms of each case appear on page 127.

Compound subjects and objects: *she and I* vs. *her and me*

Subjects° and objects° consisting of two or more nouns and pronouns have the same case forms as they would if one pronoun stood alone.

compound subject
She and Clinton discussed the proposal.

compound object
The proposal disappointed *her and him*.

To test for the correct form, try one pronoun alone in the sentence. The case form that sounds correct is probably correct for all parts of the compound.

The prize went to (*he, him*) and (*I, me*).
The prize went to *him*.
The prize went to *him and me*.

Subject complements: *it was she*

Both a subject and a subject complement° are in the subjective case.

subject
complement
The one who cares most is *she*.

If this construction sounds stilted to you, use the more natural order: <u>She</u> *is the one who cares most*.

Who vs. *whom*

The choice between *who* and *whom* depends on the use of the word.

Questions

At the beginning of a question use *who* for a subject and *whom* for an object.

subject ⤸   object ⤶
Who wrote the policy? *Whom* does it affect?

Test for the correct form by answering the question with the form of *he* or *she* that sounds correct. Then use the same case in the question.

(*Who, Whom*) does one ask?
One asks *her*.
Whom does one ask?

Subordinate clauses

In subordinate clauses° use *who* and *whoever* for all subjects, *whom* and *whomever* for all objects.

subject ⤸
Give old clothes to *whoever* needs them.
object ⤶
I don't know *whom* the major appointed.

Test for the correct form by rewriting the subordinate clause as a sentence. Replace *who* or *whom* with the form of *he* or *she* that sounds correct. Then use the same case in the original subordinate clause.

Few people know (*who, whom*) they should ask.
They should ask *her*.
Few people know *whom* they should ask.

NOTE: Don't let expressions such as *I think* and *she says* confuse you when they come between the subject *who* and its verb.

subject ⤸
He is the one *who* I think is best qualified.

Other constructions

We or *us* with a noun

The choice of *we* or *us* before a noun depends on the use of the noun.

object of
preposition
Freezing weather is welcomed by *us* skaters.
subject ⤸
We skaters welcome freezing weather.

Pronoun in an appositive

In an appositive° the case of a pronoun depends on the function of the word the appositive describes or identifies.

object of verb

The class elected two representatives, DeShawn and *me*.

subject

Two representatives, DeShawn and *I*, were elected.

Pronoun after *than* or *as*

14

After *than* or *as* in a comparison, the case of a pronoun indicates what words may have been omitted. A subjective pronoun must be the subject of the omitted verb:

subject

Annie liked Nancy more than *he* (liked Nancy).

An objective pronoun must be the object of the omitted verb:

object

Annie liked Nancy more than (Annie liked) *him*.

Subject and object of an infinitive

Both the object *and* the subject of an infinitive° are in the objective case.

subject of
infinitive

The school asked *him* to speak.

object of
infinitive

Students chose to invite *him*.

Case before a gerund

Ordinarily, use the possessive form of a pronoun or noun immediately before a gerund.°

The coach disapproved of *their* lifting weights.

The *coach's* disapproving was a surprise.

14

AGREEMENT OF PRONOUN AND ANTECEDENT

The ANTECEDENT of a pronoun° is the noun° or other pronoun it refers to.

Home owners fret over *their* tax bills.

antecedent   pronoun

Its amount makes the *tax bill* a dreaded document.
pronoun   antecedent

For clarity, a pronoun should agree with its antecedent in person,° number,° and gender.°

Antecedents with *and*

The dean and my adviser have offered *their* help.

NOTE: When *each* or *every* precedes the compound antecedent, the pronoun is singular.

Every girl and woman took *her* seat.

Antecedents with *or* or *nor*

When parts of an antecedent are joined by *or* or *nor,* the pronoun agrees with the nearer part.

Tenants or owners must present *their* grievances.

Either the tenant or the owner will have *her* way.

When one subject is plural and the other singular, the sentence will be awkward unless you put the plural one second.

AWKWARD   Neither the tenants nor the owner has yet made *her* case.

REVISED   Neither the owner nor the tenants have yet made *their* case.

Everyone and other indefinite pronouns

Most indefinite pronouns,° such as *anybody* and *everyone,* are singular in meaning. When they serve as antecedents to other pronouns, the other pronouns ar also singular.

Everyone on the team had *her* own locker.

Each of the boys likes *his* teacher.

NOTE: Tradition has called for *he* to refer to indefinite pronouns and other indefinite words (*child, adult, individual, person*), even when both masculine and feminine genders are intended. But increasingly this so-called generic (or generalized) *he* is considered inaccurate or unfair because it excludes females. To avoid it, try one of the following techniques.

GENERIC *HE*   Nobody in the class had the credits *he* needed.

- Substitute *he or she*.

    REVISED   Nobody in the class had the credits *he or she* needed.

    To avoid awkwardness, don't use *he or she* more than once in several sentences.

- Recast the sentence using a plural antecedent and pronoun.

    REVISED   *All the students* in the class lacked the credits *they* needed.

- Rewrite the sentence to avoid the pronoun.

    REVISED   Nobody in the class had the *needed credits*.

Team and other collective nouns

Use a singular pronoun with *team, family, group,* or another collective noun° when referring to the group as a unit.

The committee voted to disband *itself*.

When referring to the individual members of the group, use a plural pronoun.

The old group have gone *their* separate ways.

15

REFERENCE OF PRONOUN
TO ANTECEDENT

If a pronoun° does not refer clearly to the word it substitutes for (its ANTECEDENT), readers will have difficulty grasping the pronoun's meaning.

Single antecedent

When either of two words can be a pronoun's antecedent, the reference will not be clear.

CONFUSING   The workers removed all the furniture from the room and cleaned *it*.

Revise such a sentence in one of two ways:

• Replace the pronoun with the appropriate noun.

CLEAR   The workers removed all the furniture from the room and cleaned *the room* (or *the furniture*).

• Avoid repetition by rewriting the sentence with the pronoun but with only one possible antecedent.

CLEAR   After removing all the furniture from *it,* the workers cleaned the room.

CLEAR   The workers cleaned all the furniture after removing *it* from the room.

Close antecedent

A clause beginning *who, which,* or *that* should generally fall immediately after the word it refers to.

CONFUSING   Jody found a dress in the attic *that* her aunt had worn.

CLEAR   In the attic Jody found a dress *that* her aunt had worn.

Specific antecedent

A pronoun should refer to a specific noun° or other pronoun.

Vague *this, that, which,* or *it*

This, that, which, or *it* should refer to a specific noun, not to a whole word group expressing an idea or situation.

CONFUSING	The British knew little of the American countryside and had no experience with the colonists' guerrilla tactics. *This* gave the colonists an advantage.
CLEAR	The British knew little of the American countryside and had no experience with the colonists' guerrilla tactics. This *ignorance and inexperience* gave the colonists an advantage.

Implied nouns

A pronoun cannot refer clearly to a noun that is merely implied by some other word or phrase, such as *news* in *newspaper* or *happiness* in *happy*.

CONFUSING	In the speaker's advice *she* was not specific.
CLEAR	The *speaker's advice* was not specific.
CONFUSING	She spoke once before, but *it* was sparsely attended.
CLEAR	She spoke once before, but *the speech* was sparsely attended.

Indefinite *it* and *they*

It and *they* should have definite antecedents.

CONFUSING	In the average television drama *they* present a false picture of life.
CLEAR	The average television *drama* presents a false picture of life.

Consistency in pronouns

Within a sentence or a group of related sentences, pronouns should be consistent.

INCONSISTENT	*One* finds when reading that *your* concentration improves with practice, so that *I* now comprehend more in less time.
REVISED	*I* find when reading that *my* concentration improves with practice, so that I now comprehend more in less time.

MODIFIERS

16
ADJECTIVES AND ADVERBS

ADJECTIVES modify nouns° (*happy child*) and pronouns° (*special someone*). ADVERBS modify verbs° (*almost see*), adjectives (*very happy*), other adverbs (*not very*), and whole word groups (*Otherwise, the room was empty*). The only way to tell if a modifier should be an adjective or an adverb is to determine its function in the sentence.

Adjective vs. adverb

Use only adverbs, not adjectives, to modify verbs, adverbs, or other adjectives.

NOT   They took each other *serious*.

BUT   They took each other *seriously*.

Adjective with linking verb: *felt bad*

A modifier after a verb should be an adjective if it describes the subject,° an adverb if it describes the verb. In the first example below, the linking verb° connects the subject and an adjective describing the subject.

The sailors felt *bad*.
     linking adjective
     verb

Some sailors fare *badly* in rough weather.
       verb adverb

Good and *well* are frequently confused after verbs.

Decker trained *well*. [Adverb.]
She felt *well*. Her prospects were *good*. [Adjectives.]

Comparison of adjectives and adverbs

Comparison° allows adjectives and adverbs to show degrees of quality or amount by changing form: *red, redder, red-*

dest; awful, more awful, most awful; quickly, less quickly, least quickly. A dictionary will list the *-er* and *-est* endings if they can be used. Otherwise, use *more* and *most* or *less* and *least*.

Some modifiers are irregular, changing their spelling for comparison: for example, *good, better, best; many, more, most; badly, worse, worst.*

Double comparisons

A double comparison combines the *-er* or *-est* ending with the word *more* or *most*. It is redundant.

16

Chang was the *wisest* (not *most wisest*) person in town.
He was *smarter* (not *more smarter*) than anyone else.

Complete comparisons

A comparison should be complete.

• The comparison should state a relation fully enough to ensure clarity.

UNCLEAR	Car makers worry about their industry more than environmentalists.
CLEAR	Car makers worry about their industry more than environmentalists *do.*
CLEAR	Car makers worry about their industry more than *they worry about* environmentalists.

• The items being compared should in fact be comparable.

| ILLOGICAL | The cost of an electric car is greater than a gasoline-powered car. [Illogically compares a cost and a car.] |
| REVISED | The cost of an electric car is greater than *the cost of* (or *that of*) a gasoline-powered car. |

Double negatives

A DOUBLE NEGATIVE is a nonstandard construction in which two negative words cancel each other out. For instance, *Jenny did not feel nothing* asserts that Jenny felt other than nothing, or *something*.

| FAULTY | We could *not hardly* hear the speaker. *None* of her ideas *never* made it to the back of the room. |
| REVISED | We could *hardly* hear the speaker. *None* of her ideas made it to the back of the room. |

REVISED   We could *not* hear the speaker. Her ideas *never* made it to the back of the room.

Present and past participles as adjectives   ESL

Both present paticiples° and past participles° may serve as adjectives: *a burning bush, a burned bush.* As in the examples, the two participles usually differ in the time they indicate.

But some present and past participles—those derived from verbs expressing feeling—can have altogether different meanings. The present participle refers to something that causes the feeling: *That was a frightening storm.* The past participle refers to something that experiences the feeling: *They quieted the frightened horses.* Similar pairs include the following: *annoying/annoyed, boring/bored, confusing/confused, exciting/excited, exhausting/exhausted, fascinating/fascinated, interesting/interested, pleasing/pleased, satisfying/satisfied, surprising/surprised, tiring/tired, worrying/worried.*

Articles: *a, an, the*   ESL

Articles° usually trouble native English speakers only in the choice of *a* versus *an: a* for words beginning with consonant sounds (*a bridge, a uniform), an* for words beginning with vowel sounds, including silent *h*'s (*an apple, an urge, an hour*).

For nonnative speakers, *a, an,* and *the* can be difficult, because many other languages use such words quite differently. In English, their uses depend on the kinds of nouns they precede and the context they appear in.

Singular count nouns

A COUNT NOUN is a singular noun that names something countable and can form a plural: *glass/glasses, child/children.*

• *A* or *an* precedes a singular count noun when the reader does not already know its identity, usually because you have not mentioned it before.

A scientist in our chemistry department developed *a* process to strengthen metals. [*Scientist* and *process* are being introduced for the first time.]

• *The* precedes a singular count noun that has a specific identity for the reader, usually because (1) you have mentioned it before or (2) you identify it immediately before or after you state it.

A scientist in our chemistry department developed a process to strengthen metals. *The* scientist patented *the* process. [*Scientist* and *process* were identified in the preceding sentence.]

The most productive laboratory is *the* research center in the chemistry department. [*Most productive* identifies *laboratory,* and *in the chemistry department* identifies *research center.*]

Plural nouns

16

A or *an* never precedes a plural noun. *The* does not precede a plural noun that names a general category. *The* does precede a plural noun that names specific representatives of a category.

Men and *women* are different. [*Men* and *women* name general categories.]

The women formed a team. [*Women* refers to specific people.]

Mass nouns

A MASS NOUN is a singular noun that names something not usually considered countable in English, such as *advice, cereal, confidence, furniture, health, honesty, information, lumber, mail, oil, pollution, research, silver, truth, water, work.*

A or *an* never precedes a mass noun. *The* does precede a mass noun that names specific representatives of a general category.

Vegetation suffers from drought. [*Vegetation* names a general category.]

The vegetation in the park withered or died. [*Vegetation* refers to specific plants.]

NOTE: Many nouns are sometimes count nouns and sometimes mass nouns.

The library has *a room* for readers. [*Room* is a count noun meaning "walled area."]

The library has *room* for reading. [*Room* is a mass noun meaning "space."]

Proper nouns

A PROPER NOUN names a particular person, place, or thing and begins with a capital letter: *February, Joe Allen. A* or *an* never precedes a proper noun. *The* rarely does.

Garcia lives in *Boulder,* where he attends *the University of Colorado.*

17
MISPLACED AND DANGLING MODIFIERS

For clarity, modifiers generally must fall close to the words they modify.

Misplaced modifiers

A MISPLACED MODIFIER falls in the wrong place in a sentence. It may be awkward, confusing, or even unintentionally funny.

Clear placement

CONFUSING   He served steak to the men *on paper plates.*

REVISED   He served the men steak *on paper plates.*

CONFUSING   Many dogs are killed by automobiles and trucks *roaming unleashed.*

REVISED   Many dogs *roaming unleashed* are killed by automobiles and trucks.

Only and other limiting modifiers

LIMITING MODIFIERS include *almost, even, exactly, hardly, just, merely, nearly, only, scarcely,* and *simply.* They should fall immediately before the word or word group they modify.

UNCLEAR   They *only* saw each other during meals.

REVISED   They saw *only* each other during meals.

REVISED   They saw each other *only* during meals.

Infinitives and other grammatical units

Some grammatical units should generally not be split by long modifiers. For example, a long modifier between subject° and verb° can be awkward and confusing.

AWKWARD   The *wreckers,* soon after they began demolishing the old house, *discovered* a large box of coins.

REVISED   Soon after they began demolishing the old house, the *wreckers discovered* a large box of coins.

A split infinitive°—a modifier placed between *to* and the verb—can be especially awkward and annoys many readers.

↙ infinitive ↘

AWKWARD   Forecasters expected temperatures *to* not *rise*.

infinitive

REVISED   Forecasters expected temperatures not *to rise*.

A split infinitive may sometimes be natural and preferable, though it may still bother some readers.

↙——infinitive——↘

Several U.S. industries expect *to* more than *triple* their use of robots.

Order of adjectives ESL

English follows distinctive rules for arranging two or three adjectives before a noun. (A string of more than three adjectives before a noun is rare.) Adjectives always precede the noun except when they are subject complements,° and they follow this order:

1. Article or other word marking the noun: *a, an, the, this, Mary's*
2. Word of opinion: *beautiful, disgusting, important, fine*
3. Word about measurement: *small, huge, short, towering*
4. Word about shape: *round, flat, square, triangular*
5. Word about age: *old, young, new, ancient*
6. Word about color: *green, white, black, magenta*
7. Word about origin (nationality, religion, etc.): *European, Iranian, Jewish, Parisian*
8. Word about material: *wooden, gold, nylon, stone*

Examples of this order include *a gorgeous blue sky, Kim's tiny glass beads, the new Italian fashions.*

Dangling modifiers

A DANGLING MODIFIER does not sensibly modify anything in its sentence.

————→ ⊘

DANGLING   *Passing the building,* the vandalism became visible.

Like most dangling modifiers, this one introduces a sentence, contains a verb form° (*passing*), and implies but does not name a subject (the someone or something passing the building). Readers assume that this implied subject is the same as the subject of the sentence (*vandalism*). When it is not, the modifier "dangles" unconnected to the rest of the sentence.

44 . Misplaced and dangling modifiers

Revise dangling modifiers to achieve the emphasis you want.

- Rewrite the dangling modifier as a complete clause with its own stated subject and verb. Readers can accept that the new subject and the sentence subject are different.

DANGLING   *Passing the building,* the vandalism became visible.

REVISED   *As we passed* the building, the vandalism became visible.

- Change the subject of the sentence to a word the modifier properly describes.

DANGLING   *Trying to understand the causes,* vandalism has been extensively studied.

REVISED   Trying to understand the causes, *researchers have* extensively *studied* vandalism.

SENTENCE FAULTS

18

SENTENCE FRAGMENTS

A SENTENCE FRAGMENT is part of a sentence that is set off as if it were a whole sentence by an initial capital letter and a final period or other end punctuation. Although writers occasionally use fragments deliberately and effectively, most fragments are serious errors in standard English.

NOTE ESL   Some languages other than English allow the omission of the subject° or verb.° Except in commands (*Close the door*), English always requires you to state the subject and verb.

Tests for fragments

A word group punctuated as a sentence should pass *all three* of the following tests. If it does not, it is a fragment and needs to be revised.

Test 1: Find the verb.

The verb in a complete sentence can change form as indicated on the left below. A verb form° that cannot change this way (as on the right) cannot serve as a sentence verb.

	COMPLETE SENTENCES	SENTENCE FRAGMENTS
SINGULAR	The baboon *looks*.	The baboon *looking*.
PLURAL	The baboons *look*.	The baboons *looking*.
PRESENT	The baboon *looks*.	
PAST	The baboon *looked*.	The baboon *looking*.
FUTURE	The baboon *will look*.	

Test 2: Find the subject.

The subject of the sentence will usually come before the verb. If there is no subject, the word group is probably a fragment.

FRAGMENT	And eyed the guard nervously.
REVISED	And *he* eyed the guard nervously.

Test 3: Make sure the clause is not subordinate.

A subordinate clause° begins with either a subordinating conjunction° (such as *because, if, when*) or a relative pronoun° (*who, which, that*). Subordinate clauses serve as parts of sentences, not as whole sentences.

| FRAGMENT | When the next cage rattled. |
| REVISED | The next cage rattled. |

NOTE: Questions beginning *who, whom,* or *which* are not sentence fragments: *Who rattled the cage?*

Revision of fragments

Correct sentence fragments in one of two ways depending on the importance of the information in the fragment.

- As in all examples so far, rewrite the fragment as a complete sentence. The information in the fragment will then have the same importance as that in other complete sentences.
- Combine the fragment with the appropriate main clause. The information in the fragment will then be subordinated to that in the main clause.

| FRAGMENT | The challenger was a newcomer. *Who was unusually fierce.* |
| REVISED | The challenger was a newcomer who was unusually fierce. |

19

COMMA SPLICES AND FUSED SENTENCES

When two complete sentences (main clauses°) combine in one sentence, readers need a clear signal that one clause is ending and the other beginning. In a COMMA SPLICE two main clauses are joined (or spliced) only by a comma, which is usually too weak a signal.

| COMMA SPLICE | The ship was huge, its mast stood eighty feet high. |

In a FUSED SENTENCE the clauses are not separated at all.

FUSED SENTENCE   The ship was huge its mast stood eighty feet high.

Main clauses without *and, but, or, nor, for, so, yet*

And, but, or, or another coordinating conjunction° often signals the joining of main clauses. Revise sentences that lack this signal in one of the following ways:

- Make the clauses into separate sentences when the ideas expressed are only loosely related.

COMMA SPLICE   Chemistry has contributed much to our understanding of foods, many foods such as wheat and beans can be produced in the laboratory.

REVISED   Chemistry has contributed much to our understanding of foods**.** Many foods such as wheat and beans can be produced in the laboratory.

- Insert a coordinating conjunction when the ideas in the main clauses are closely related and equally important.

COMMA SPLICE   Some laboratory-grown foods taste good, they are nutritious.

REVISED   Some laboratory-grown foods taste good**,** *and* they are nutritious.

In a fused sentence insert a comma and a coordinating conjunction.

FUSED   Chemists have made much progress they still have a way to go.

REVISED   Chemists have made much progress**,** *but* they still have a way to go.

- Insert a semicolon between clauses if the relation between the ideas is very close and obvious without a conjunction.

COMMA SPLICE   Good taste is rare in laboratory-grown vegetables, they are usually bland.

REVISED   Good taste is rare in laboratory-grown vegetables**;** they are usually bland.

- Subordinate one clause to the other when one idea is less

important than the other. The subordinated element will modify something in the main clause.

COMMA SPLICE	The vitamins are adequate, the flavor and color are deficient.
REVISED	*Even though* the vitamins are adequate, the flavor and color are deficient.

Main clauses related by *however, thus,* or another conjunctive adverb

Conjunctive adverbs° such as *however, instead, meanwhile, therefore,* and *thus* describe how one clause relates to another. Two clauses related by a conjunctive adverb must be separated by a period or by a semicolon. The adverb is also generally set off by a comma or commas.

COMMA SPLICE	Most Americans refuse to give up unhealthful habits, consequently our medical costs are higher than those of many other countries.
REVISED	Most Americans refuse to give up unhealthful habits. *Consequently,* our medical costs are higher than those of many other countries.
REVISED	Most Americans refuse to give up unhealthful habits; *consequently,* our medical costs are higher than those of many other countries.

To test whether a word is a conjunctive adverb, try repositioning it in its clause. It can move.

Most Americans refuse to give up unhealthful habits; our medical costs, *consequently,* are higher than those of many other countries.

III

PUNCTUATION

20

END PUNCTUATION

End a sentence with one of three punctuation marks: a period, a question mark, or an exclamation point.

Period for most sentences and many abbreviations

Statements	Mild commands
The airline went bankrupt.	Think of the possibilities.
It no longer flies.	Please consider others.

Indirect questions°

The judge asked why I had been driving with my lights off.
No one asked how we got home.

Abbreviations

p.	B.C.	B.A.	Mr.
M.D.	A.D.	Ph.D.	Mrs.
Dr.	A.M., a.m.	e.g.	Ms.
St.	P.M., p.m.	i.e.	

Omit periods from most abbreviations of three or more words:

IBM	JFK
USMC	VISTA

Question mark for direct questions°

Who will follow her?
What is the difference between these two people?

Exclamation point for strong statements and commands

No! We must not lose this election!
"Oh!" she gasped.
Come here immediately!

NOTE: Use exclamation points sparingly, even in informal writing. They can make writing sound overly dramatic.

21
THE COMMA

The comma is the most common punctuation mark inside sentences. Its main uses (and misuses) appear below.

With *and, but, or, nor, for, so, yet*

Use a comma before *and, but, or, nor, for, so,* and *yet* (the coordinating conjunctions°) when they link complete sentences (main clauses°).

> Banks offer many services to customers, *but* they could do more.

> Many banks offer investment advice, *and* they help small businesses establish credit.

Generally, do not use a comma before *and, but, or,* and *nor* when they link structures other than complete sentences.

NOT One bank *established* special accounts for older depositors, *and counseled* them on investments.

BUT One bank established special accounts for older depositors and counseled them on investments.

With introductory elements

Use a comma after most elements that begin sentences and modify something in the rest of the sentence.

> *When a new century nears,* futurists multiply.
> *Fortunately,* some news is good.

You may omit the comma after short introductory elements if there's no risk of misreading: <u>By the year 2000</u> *we may have reduced pollution.*

With interrupting and concluding elements

Use a comma or commas to set off elements that provide nonessential information—information that could be deleted without altering the basic meaning of the sentence or leaving it too general. When the information falls in the middle of the sentence, be sure to use one comma *before* and one *after* it.

Nonrestrictive elements°

Hai Nguyen, *who emigrated from Vietnam*, lives in Denver.

His work, *research for an environmental company*, keeps him in Denver.

The company, *which is ten years old*, studies air pollution.

Nguyen's family lives in St. Louis and Chicago, *even though he lives in Denver.*

Absolute phrases°

Nguyen, *his family scattered*, requested a flexible schedule.

Parenthetical expressions°

Most employees, *it seems*, do not have enough flexibility in their work week.

Phrases of contrast

Nguyen's company values the quality of his work, *not just the quantity.*

Yes and *no*

The company decided that, *yes*, Nguyen could develop a more flexible work schedule.

Words of direct address

Heed this lesson, *readers.*

Do not use commas to set off *essential* information—information that cannot be omitted without leaving the meaning unclear or too general.

Restrictive elements°

People *who join recycling programs* rarely complain about the extra work.

The programs *that succeed* are often staffed by volunteers.

The label *"Recycle"* on products becomes a command.

Most people recycle *because they believe they have a responsibility to the earth.*

With series

Use commas to separate the items in lists, or series.

The names *Belial, Beelzebub, and Lucifer* sound ominous.

The comma before the last item in a series (before *and*) is actually optional, but it is never wrong and it is usually clearer.

Do not use commas *around* series.

Nor The skills of, *agriculture, herding, and hunting,* sustained the Native Americans.

But The skills of agriculture, herding, and hunting sustained the Native Americans.

With adjectives

Use a comma between adjectives° that modify the same word equally. As a test, such adjectives could be joined by *and*.

The *dirty, dented* car was a neighborhood eyesore.

Do not use a comma between adjectives when one forms a unit with the modified word. As a test, the two adjectives could not sensibly be joined by *and*.

The house overflowed with *ornate electric* fixtures.
Among the junk in the attic was *one lovely* vase.

With dates, addresses, place names, numbers

When they appear within sentences, elements punctuated with commas are also ended with commas.

Dates

July 4, 1776, was the day the Declaration was signed. [Note that commas appear before *and* after the year.]

The United States entered World War II in December 1941. [No comma is needed between a month or season and a year.]

Addresses and place names

Use the address 806 Ogden Avenue, Swarthmore, Pennsylvania 19081, for all correspondence. [No comma is needed between the state name and zip code.]

Numbers

The new assembly plant cost $7,525,000.
A kilometer is 3,281 feet (*or* 3281 feet).

With quotations

A comma or commas usually separate a quotation from the words used to identify the source, such as *she said* or *he replied.*

> Eleanor Roosevelt said, "You must do the thing you think you cannot do."

> "Knowledge is power," wrote Francis Bacon.

> "You don't need a weatherman," sings Bob Dylan, "to know which way the wind blows."

Do not use a comma when identifying words interrupt the quotation between main clauses.° Instead, follow the identifying words with a semicolon or period.

> "That part of my life was over," she wrote; "his words had sealed it shut."

> "That part of my life was over," she wrote. "His words had sealed it shut."

22

THE SEMICOLON

The semicolon separates equal and balanced sentence elements.

Between complete sentences

Use a semicolon between complete sentences (main clauses°) that are not connected by *and, but, or, nor, for, so,* or *yet* (the coordinating conjunctions°).

> Increased taxes are only one way to pay for programs; cost cutting also frees up money.

Do not use a semicolon between a main clause and a subordinate element, such as a subordinate clause° or a phrase.°

> Not   According to African authorities; only about 35,000 Pygmies exist today.

BUT	According to African authorities, only about 35,000 Pygmies exist today.
NOT	Anthropologists have campaigned; for the protection of the Pygmies' habitat.
BUT	Anthropologists have campaigned for the protection of the Pygmies' habitat.

With *however, thus,* etc.

Use a semicolon between complete sentences (main clauses°) that are related by a conjunctive adverb° such as *hence, however, indeed, moreover, therefore,* and *thus.*

22

Blue jeans have become fashionable all over the world; *however,* the American originators still wear more jeans than anyone else.

A conjunctive adverb may move around within its clause, so the semicolon will not always come just before the adverb. The adverb itself is usually set off with a comma or commas.

Blue jeans have become fashionable all over the word; the American originators, *however,* still wear more jeans than anyone else.

With series

Use semicolons (rather than commas) to separate items in a series when the items contain commas.

The custody case involved Amy Dalton, the child; Ellen and Mark Dalton, the parents; and Ruth and Hal Blum, the grandparents.

Do not use a semicolon to introduce a series. (Use a colon or a dash instead.)

NOT	Teachers have heard all sorts of reasons why students do poorly; psychological problems, family illness, too much work, too little time.
BUT	Teachers have heard all sorts of reasons why students do poorly: psychological problems, family illness, too much work, too little time.

23

THE COLON

The colon is mainly a mark of introduction, but it has a few other conventional uses as well.

For introduction

The colon ends a complete sentence (main clause°) and introduces various additions:

Soul food has a deceptively simple definition: the ethnic cooking of African-Americans.

At least three soul food dishes are familiar to most Americans: fried chicken, barbecued spareribs, and sweet potatoes.

Soul food has one disadvantage: fat.

One soul food chef has a solution: "Instead of using ham hocks to flavor beans, I use smoked turkey wings. The soulful, smoky taste remains, but without all the fat of pork."

Do not use a colon inside a main clause, especially after *such as* or a verb.

NOT The best-known soul food dish is: fried chicken. Many Americans have not tasted delicacies such as: chitlins and black-eyed peas.

BUT The best-known soul food dish is fried chicken. Many Americans have not tasted declicacies such as chitlins and black-eyed peas.

With salutations of business letters, titles and subtitles, divisions of time, and biblical citations

Salutation of a business letter
Dear Ms. Burak:

Title and subtitle
Anna Freud: Her Life and Work

Time		Biblical citation
12:26	6:00	1 Corinthians 3:6-7

24
THE APOSTROPHE

The apostrophe appears as part of a word to indicate possession, the omission of one or more letters, or (in a few cases) plural number.

With possessives

NOTE: The apostrophe or apostrophe-plus-*s* is an *addition.* Before this addition, always spell the name of the owner or owners without dropping or adding letters.

Singular words: Add -'s

Bill *Boughton's* skillful card tricks amaze children.
Anyone's eyes would widen.

The *-'s* ending for singular words pertains to singular words ending in *-s.*

Sandra *Cisneros's* work is highly regarded.
The *business's* customers filed suit.

Plural words ending in -s: Add -' only

Workers' incomes have fallen slightly over the past year.
Many students take several *years'* leave after high school.
The *Murphys'* son lives at home.

Plural words not ending in -s: Add -'s

Children's educations are at stake.
We need to attract the *media's* attention.

Compound words: Add -'s only to the last word

The *brother-in-law's* business failed.
Taxes are always *somebody else's* fault.

Two or more owners: Add -'s depending on possession

Youngman's and Mason's comedy techniques are similar.
[Each comedian has his own technique.]

The child recovered despite her *mother and father's* neglect.
[The mother and father were jointly neglectful.]

Misuses

Plural nouns°

Not   The unleashed *dog's* belonged to the *Jones'*.

But   The unleased *dogs* belonged to the *Joneses*.

Singular verbs°

Not   The subway *break's* down less often now.

But   The subway *breaks* down less often now.

Possessives of personal pronouns°

Not   The car is *her's*, not *their's*. *It's* color is red.

But   The car is *hers*, not *theirs*. *Its* color is red.

Note: Don't confuse possessive pronouns and contractions: *its, your, their,* and *whose* are possessives. *It's, you're, they're,* and *who's* are contractions. See below.

With contractions

A CONTRACTION replaces one or more letters, numbers, or words with an apostrophe.

it is	it's	cannot	can't
you are	you're	does not	doesn't
they are	they're	were not	weren't
who is	who's	class of 1997	class of '97

Note: Don't misuse the four contractions on the left for the possessive pronouns° *its, their, your,* and *whose.*

With plural letters, numbers, and words named as words

You may cite a character or word as a word rather than use it for its meaning. When such an element is plural, add an apostrophe plus -*s*.

This sentence has too many <u>but</u>'s.
Remember to dot your <u>i</u>'s and cross your <u>t</u>'s.
At the end of each poem, the author had written two <u>3</u>'s.

Notice that cited element is underlined (italicized) but the apostrophe and added -*s* are not.

25

QUOTATION MARKS

Quotation marks—either double (" ") or single (' ')—mainly enclose direct quotations from speech and from writing. They *always* come in pairs.

With direct quotations

A DIRECT QUOTATION reports what someone said or wrote, in the exact words of the original.

> "Life," said the psychoanalyst Karen Horney, "remains a very efficient therapist."

Do not use quotation marks with an INDIRECT QUOTATION, which reports what someone said or wrote but not in the exact words of the original.

Use single quotation marks to enclose a quotation within a quotation.

> "In formulating any philosophy," Woody Allen writes, "the first consideration must always be: What can we know? . . . Descartes hinted at the problem when he wrote, 'My mind can never know my body, although it has become quite friendly with my leg.' "

With titles of works

Use quotation marks to enclose the titles of works that are published or released within larger works (see below). Use underlining (italics) for all other titles (see p. 74).

Song
"Satisfaction"

Essay
"Joey: A 'Mechanical Boy'"

Short story
"The Gift of the Magi"

Episode of a television or radio program
"The Mexican Connection" (on <u>Sixty Minutes</u>)

Short poem
"Her Kind"

Article in a periodical
"Does 'Scaring' Work?"

Subdivision of a book
"The Mast Head" (Chapter 35 of <u>Moby Dick</u>)

With defined words

By "charity" I mean the love of one's neighbor as oneself.

NOTE: Underlining (italics) may also highlight defined words.

With other punctuation

Commas and periods: inside quotation marks

Jonathan Swift wrote a famous satire, "A Modest Proposal," in 1729.

"Swift's 'A Modest Proposal,' " wrote one critic, "is so outrageous that it cannot be believed."

Colons and semicolons: outside quotation marks

A few years ago the slogan in elementary education was "learning by playing"; now educators focus on basic skills.

We all know the meaning of "basic skills": reading, writing, and arithmetic.

Dashes, question marks, and exclamation points: inside quotation marks only if part of the quotation

When a dash, question mark, or exclamation point is part of the quotation, place it *inside* quotation marks. Don't use any other punctuation, such as a period or comma.

"But must you—" Marcia hesitated, afraid of the answer.
The stranger asked, "Where am I?"
"Go away!" I yelled.

When a dash, question mark, or exclamation point applies only to the larger sentence, not to the quotation, place it *outside* quotation marks—again, with no other punctuation.

Betty Friedan's question in 1963—"Who knows what women can be?"—encouraged generations of women to seek answers.

Who said, "Now cracks a noble heart"?

The woman called me "stupid"!

When both the quotation and the larger sentence take a question mark or exclamation point, use only the one *inside* the quotation mark.

Did you say, "Who is she?"

26
OTHER MARKS

The other marks of punctuation are the dash, parentheses, the ellipsis mark, brackets, and the slash.

Dash or dashes for shifts and interruptions

In handwritten and typewritten papers, form a dash with two hyphens (--). Do not add extra space before, after, or between the hyphens.

Shifts in tone or thought

He tells us—does he really mean it?—that he will speak the truth from now on.

If she found out—he did not want to think what she would do.

Nonessential elements

Dashes may be used instead of commas to set off and emphasize elements that are not essential to the meaning of the sentence. Be sure to use a pair of dashes when the element interrupts the sentence.

The qualities Monet painted—sunlight, rich shadows, deep colors—abounded near the rivers and gardens he used as subjects.

Introductory series and concluding series and explanations

Shortness of breath, skin discoloration or the sudden appearance of moles, persistent indigestion, the presence of small lumps—all these may signify cancer. [Introductory series.]

The patient undergoes a battery of tests—CAT scan, bronchoscopy, perhaps even biopsy. [Concluding series.]

Many patients are disturbed by the CAT scan—by the need to keep still for long periods in an exceedingly small space. [Concluding explanation.]

A colon could be used instead of a dash in the last two examples. The dash is more informal.

26

Parentheses for nonessential elements

Parentheses always come in pairs, one before and one after
the punctuated material.

Parenthetical expressions

Parentheses de-emphasize PARENTHETICAL EXPRESSIONS—
explanatory, supplemental, or transitional words or phrases.
(Commas emphasize these expressions more and dashes still
more.)

> The population of Philadelphia (now about 1.6 million) has
> declined since 1950.

Don't put a comma before a parenthetical expression enclosed in parentheses. Punctuation after the parenthetical expression should be placed outside the closing parenthesis.

> NOT We were haunted by the dungeon, (really the basement.)
>
> BUT We were haunted by the dungeon (really the basement).

Labels for lists

> My father could not, for his own special reasons, even *like* me.
> He spent the first twenty-five years of my life acting out that
> painful fact. Then he arrived at two points in his own life: **(1)**
> his last years, and **(2)** the realization that he had made a tragic
> mistake.   —RAY WEATHERLY

Ellipsis mark for omissions from quotations

The ellipsis mark consists of three spaced periods (. . .). It
generally indicates an omission from a quotation, as illustrated
in the following excerpts from this quotation about the Philippines:

ORIGINAL QUOTATION

> "It was the Cuba of the future. It was going the way of Iran. It
> was another Nicaragua, another Cambodia, another Vietnam.
> But all these places, awesome in their histories, are so different
> from each other that one couldn't help thinking: this kind of
> talk was shorthand for a confusion. All that was being said was
> that something was happening in the Philippines. Or more
> plausibly, a lot of different things were happening in the Phil-
> ippines. And a lot of people were feeling obliged to speak out
> about it."   —JAMES FENTON, "The Philippine Election"

26

OMISSION OF THE MIDDLE OF A SENTENCE

"But all these places **. . .** are so different from each other that one couldn't help thinking: this kind of talk was a shorthand for a confusion."

OMISSION OF THE END OF A SENTENCE

"It was another Nicaragua. **. . .**" [Note the sentence period preceding the ellipsis mark.]

OMISSION OF PARTS OF TWO SENTENCES

"All that was being said was that **. . .** a lot of different things were happening in the Philippines."

OMISSION OF ONE OR MORE SENTENCES

"It was the Cuba of the future. It was going the way of Iran. It was another Nicaragua, another Cambodia, another Vietnam. **. . .** All that was being said was that something was happening in the Philippines."

26

If you omit one or more lines of poetry or paragraphs of prose from a quotation, use a separate line of ellipsis marks across the full width of the quotation to show the omission.

Brackets for changes in quotations

Brackets have only one use: to indicate that you have altered a quotation to explain, clarify, or correct it.

"That Texaco station **[**just outside Chicago**]** is one of the busiest in the nation," said a company spokesperson.

Slash for options and between lines of poetry

Option

Some teachers oppose pass**/**fail courses.

Between lines of poetry

When you run two lines of poetry into your text, separate them with a slash surrounded by space.

Many readers have sensed a reluctant turn away from death in Frost's lines "The woods are lovely, dark and deep, **/** But I have promises to keep."

IV

CONVENTIONS OF FORM AND APPEARANCE

MANUSCRIPT FORMAT

Legible, consistent, and attractive papers and job applications are a service to your readers and reflect well on you.

Academic papers

The guidelines below are adapted from the *MLA Handbook for Writers of Research Papers*, the style book for English and some other disciplines. Most of these guidelines are standard, but instructors in various courses may expect you to follow different conventions. Check with your instructor for his or her preferences.

Materials

- Use $8\frac{1}{2}'' \times 11''$ white bond paper of sixteen- or twenty-pound weight. For handwritten manuscripts, the paper should have horizontal lines spaced about one-quarter to three-eighths inch apart.
- Use a fresh ribbon, cartridge, or pen that makes a dark impression.
- For papers produced on a word processor, make sure the printer produces legible characters. If you use continuous paper folded like a fan at perforations, remove the strips of holes along the sides, and separate the pages at the folds.

Format

The samples on the next page show the format of a paper. For the special formats of source citations and a list of works cited or references, see pages 87 (MLA style), 100 (APA style), and 107 (footnotes or endnotes).

Punctuation

Type punctuation as follows:

- Leave one space after a comma, semicolon, colon, and apostrophe closing a word.
- Leave one space after a closing quotation mark, closing parenthesis, and closing bracket when these marks fall within a sentence. When they fall after the sentence period, leave two spaces.
- Leave two spaces after a sentence period, question mark, or exclamation point.

FIRST PAGE OF PAPER

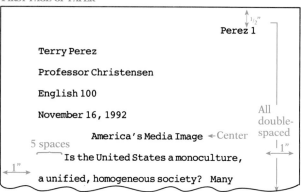

A LATER PAGE OF THE PAPER

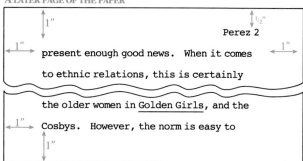

- Do not add any space before or after a dash, a hyphen, or an apostrophe within a word. Form a dash with two hyphens (--).
- Leave one space before and after an ellipsis mark (. . .).

Quotations

POETRY

- When you quote a single line from a poem, song, or verse play, run the line into your text and enclose it in quotation marks.

  Dylan Thomas remembered childhood as an idyllic time: "About the lilting house and happy as the grass was green."

- Poetry quotations of two or three lines may be placed in

the text or displayed separately. In the text enclose the quotation in quotation marks and separate the lines with a slash surrounded by space.

An example of Robert Frost's incisiveness is in two lines from "Death of the Hired Man": "Home is the place where, when you have to go there / They have to take you in."

- Quotations of more than three lines of poetry should always be separated from the text with space and an indention. *Do not add quotation marks.*

Emily Dickinson rarely needed more than a few lines to express her complex thoughts:

> To wait an Hour–is long–
> If Love be just beyond–
> To wait Eternity–is short–
> If Love reward the end–

- Double-space above, below, and throughout a displayed quotation. Indent the quotation ten spaces from the left margin.

27

PROSE

- Run a prose quotation of four or fewer typed lines into your text, and enclose it in quotation marks.
- Separate quotations of five or more typed lines from the body of your paper.

In his 1967 study of the lives of unemployed black men, Eliot Lebow observes that "unskilled" construction work requires more experience and skill than generally assumed.

> A healthy, sturdy, active man of good intelligence requires from two to four weeks to break in on a construction job. . . . It frequently happens that his foreman or the craftsman he services is not willing to wait that long for him to get into condition or to learn at a glance the difference in size between a rough 2 × 8 and a finished 2 × 10.

- Double-space before, after, and throughout a displayed quotation. *Do not add quotation marks.*

DIALOGUE

- When quoting conversations, begin a new paragraph for each speaker.

"What shall I call you? Your name?" Andrews whispered rapidly, as with a high squeak the latch of the door rose.

"Elizabeth," she said. "Elizabeth."

—GRAHAM GREENE, *The Man Within*

- When you quote a single speaker for more than one paragraph, put quotation marks at the beginning of each paragraph but at the end of only the last paragraph.

Job-application letters and résumés

Job-application letter

In a letter to a businessperson, you are addressing someone who wants to see quickly why you are writing and how to respond to you. For a job application, announce right off what job you are applying for and how you heard about it. (See the sample letter on the facing page.) Summarize your qualifications for the job, including relevant facts about your education and employment history. Include your reason for applying, such as a specific career goal. At the end of the letter mention when you are available for an interview.

Use either unlined white paper measuring $8\frac{1}{2}''\times 11''$ or what is called letterhead stationary with your address printed at the top of the sheet. Type the letter single-spaced (with double space between elements) on only one side of a sheet, following the model on the facing page.

For the salutation, which greets the addressee, use a job title (*Dear Personnel Manager*) or use a general salutation (*Dear Sir or Madam*)—unless of course you know the addressee's name. When addressing a woman by name, use *Ms.* when she has no other title, when you don't know how she prefers to be addressed, or when you know she prefers *Ms.* For the letter's close, choose an expression that reflects the formality in the salutation: *Respectfully, Cordially, Yours truly,* and *Sincerely* are more formal than *Regards* and *Best wishes.*

The envelope should show your name and address in the upper-left corner and the addressee's name, title, and address in the center. Use an envelope that will accommodate the letter once it is folded horizontally in thirds.

Résumé

The résumé that you enclose with a letter of application should contain, in table form, your name and address, career objective, and education and employment histories, along

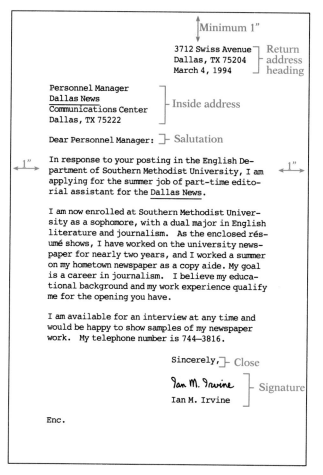

Minimum 1"

3712 Swiss Avenue ⌐ Return
Dallas, TX 75204 ⌐ address
March 4, 1994   ⌐ heading

Personnel Manager
Dallas News
Communications Center   ⌐ Inside address
Dallas, TX 75222

Dear Personnel Manager: ⌐ Salutation

1" → In response to your posting in the English De-   ← 1"
partment of Southern Methodist University, I am
applying for the summer job of part-time editorial assistant for the Dallas News.

I am now enrolled at Southern Methodist University as a sophomore, with a dual major in English
literature and journalism. As the enclosed résumé shows, I have worked on the university newspaper for nearly two years, and I worked a summer
on my hometown newspaper as a copy aide. My goal
is a career in journalism. I believe my educational background and my work experience qualify
me for the opening you have.

I am available for an interview at any time and
would be happy to show samples of my newspaper
work. My telephone number is 744-3816.

Sincerely, ⌐ Close

Ian M. Irvine
Ian M. Irvine   ⌐ Signature

Enc.

27

with information about how to obtain your references. (See the sample on the next page.) Use headings to mark the various sections of the résumé, spacing around them and within sections so that important information stands out. Try to limit your résumé to one page so that it can be quickly scanned. However, if your experience and education are extensive, a two-page résumé is preferable to a single cramped, unreadable page.

In preparing your résumé, you may wish to consult one of the many books devoted to application letters, résumés, and other elements of a job search. Two helpful guides are

Ian M. Irvine
3712 Swiss Avenue
Dallas, Texas 75204
Telephone: 214-744-3816

Position desired
Part-time editorial assistant.

Education
Southern Methodist University, 1992 to present.
Current standing: sophomore.
Major: English literature and journalism.

Abilene (Texas) Senior High School, 1988-1992.
Graduated with academic, college-preparatory
degree.

Employment history
Daily Campus, student newspaper of Southern
Methodist University, 1992 to present.
Responsibilities include writing feature stories
and sports coverage.

Longhorn Painters, summer 1993.
Responsibilities included exterior and interior
house painting.

Abilene Reporter-News, summer 1993.
Responsibilities as a copy aide included routing
copy, monitoring teleprinter, running errands,
and assisting reporters.

References
Academic: Placement Office
                   Southern Methodist University
                   Dallas, TX 75275

Employment: Ms. Millie Stevens
                   Abilene Reporter-News
                   Abilene, TX 79604

Personal: Ms. Sheryl Gipstein
                   26 Overland Drive
                   Abilene, TX 79604

27

Richard N. Bolles, *What Color Is Your Parachute? A Practical
Manual for Job-Hunters and Career Changers,* and Tom Jackson, *The Perfect Résumé.*

28
THE HYPHEN

Always use a hyphen to divide a word between syllables from one line to the next. Also use it to form some COMPOUND WORDS, such as *cross-reference*, that express a combination of ideas. The following rules cover many but not all compounds. When you doubt the spelling of a compound word, consult a dictionary.

Compound adjectives

When two or more words serve together as a single modifier° before a noun, a hyphen forms the modifying words clearly into a unit.

She is a *well-known* actor.
No *English-speaking* people were in the room.

When such a compound adjective follows the noun, the hyphen is unnecessary.

The actor is *well known*.
Those people are *English speaking*.

The hyphen is also unnecessary in a compound modifier containing an *-ly* adverb, even before the noun: *clearly defined terms*.

Fractions and compound numbers

Hyphens join the numerator and denominoator of fractions: *three-fourths, one-half*. And the whole numbers *twenty-one* to *ninety-nine* are always hyphenated.

Prefixes and suffixes

Prefixes are usually attached to word stems without hyphens: *predetermine, unnatural, disengage*. However, when the prefix precedes a capitalized word or when a capital letter is combined with a word, a hyphen usually separates the two: *un-American, A-frame*. And some prefixes, such as *self-, all-,* and *ex-* (meaning "formerly"), usually require hyphens no matter what follows: *self-control, all-inclusive, ex-student*. The only suffix that regularly requires a hyphen is *-elect*, as in *president-elect*.

28

29

CAPITAL LETTERS

The following conventions and a desk dictionary can help you decide whether to capitalize a particular word. In general, capitalize only when a rule or the dictionary says you must.

First word of a sentence

Every writer should own a good dictionary.

Proper nouns and adjectives

PROPER NOUNS name specific persons, places, and things: *Shakespeare, California, World War I.* PROPER ADJECTIVES are formed from some proper nouns: *Shakespearean, Californian.* Capitalize all proper nouns and proper adjectives but not the articles (*a, an, the*) that precede them.

Specific persons and things
Stephen King   Boulder Dam

Specific places and geographical regions
New York City   the Northeast, the South
But: northeast of the city, going south

Days of the week, months, holidays
Monday   Yom Kippur
May   Christmas

Historical events, documents, periods, movements
the Vietnam War   the Renaissance
the Constitution   the Romantic Movement

Government offices or departments and institutions
House of Representatives   Polk Municipal Court
Department of Defense   Northeast High School

Political, social, athletic, and other organizations and their members
B'nai B'rith   Democratic Party, Democrats
Rotary Club   Atlanta Falcons
League of Women Voters   Chicago Symphony Orchestra

Races, nationalities, and their languages

Native American	Germans
African-American, Negro	Swahili
Caucasian	Italian
But: blacks, whites	

Religions, their followers, and terms for the sacred

Christianity, Christians	God
Catholicism, Catholics	Allah
Judaism, Orthodox Jew	the Bible (*but* biblical)
Islam, Moslems *or* Muslims	the Koran

Also capitalize the common nouns *street, avenue, park, river, ocean, lake, company, college, county,* and *memorial* when they are part of proper nouns naming specific places or institutions.

Main Street	Lake Superior
Ventura Avenue	Ford Motor Company
Central Park	Madison College
Mississippi River	King's Country
Pacific Ocean	George Washington Memorial

29

Titles and subtitles of works

In all titles and subtitles of works, capitalize the first and last words and all other words *except* articles (*a, an the*), *to* in infinitives,° and connecting words (prepositions° and conjunctions°) of fewer than five letters. Capitalize even these short words when they are the first or last word in a title or when they fall after a colon or semicolon.

"Once More to the Lake"	*Management: A New Theory*
A Diamond Is Forever	"Courtship Through the Ages"
"Knowing Whom to Ask"	*File Under Architecture*
Learning from Las Vegas	*An End to Live For*

Titles of persons

Before a person's name, capitalize his or her title. After the name, do not capitalize the title.

Professor Otto Osborne	Otto Osborne, a professor
Doctor Jane Covington	Jane Covington, a doctor
Senator Robert Dole	Robert Dole, the senator

30
UNDERLINING (ITALICS)

Underlining and *italic type* indicate the same thing: the word or words are being distinguished or emphasized. In your papers use a ruler or the underscore on the keyboard to underline.

Titles of works

Underline the titles of works, such as books and periodicals, that are published, released, or produced separately from other works. (See below.) Use quotation marks for all other titles, such as short stories and articles in periodicals. (See p. 59.)

Book
War and Peace

Long poem
Paradise Lost

Play
Hamlet

Periodical
Philadelphia Inquirer

Pamphlet
The Truth About Alcoholism

Published speech
Lincoln's Gettysburg Address

Long musical work
The Beatles' Revolver
But: Symphony in C

Television or radio program
60 Minutes

Work of visual art
Michelangelo's David

Movie
Psycho

EXCEPTIONS: Legal documents, the Bible, and their parts are generally not underlined.

NOT We studied the Book of Revelation in the New English Bible.

BUT We studied the Book of Revelation in the New English Bible.

Ships, aircraft, spacecraft, trains

Challenger
Apollo XI

Orient Express
Montrealer

Queen Elizabeth 2
Spirit of St. Louis

Foreign Words

Underline a foreign expression that has not been absorbed into our language. A dictionary will say whether a word is still considered foreign to English.

The scientific name for the brown trout is <u>Salmo trutta</u>. [The Latin scientific names for plants and animals are always underlined.]

The Latin <u>De gustibus non est disputandum</u> translates roughly as "There's no accounting for taste."

Words, letters, and numbers named as words

Underline characters or words that are cited as words rather than used for their meanings.

Some people pronounce <u>th</u>, as in <u>thought</u>, with a faint <u>s</u> or <u>f</u> sound.

Try pronouncing <u>unique New York</u> ten times fast.

The word <u>syzygy</u> refers to a straight line formed by three celestial bodies, as in the alignment of the earth, sun, and moon. [Quotation marks may also be used for words being defined.]

31

ABBREVIATIONS

The following guidelines on abbreviations pertain to nontechnical writing. Technical writing, such as in the sciences and engineering, generally uses many more abbreviations.

Titles before and after proper names

BEFORE THE NAME	AFTER THE NAME
Dr. James Hsu	James Hsu, M.D.
Mr., Mrs., Ms., Hon.,	D.D.S., D.V.M., Ph.D.,
St., Rev., Msgr., Gen.	Ed.D., O.S.B., S.J., Sr., Jr.

Do not use abbreviations such as *Rev., Hon., Prof., Rep., Sen., Dr.,* and *St.* (for *Saint*) unless they appear before a proper name.

Familiar abbreviations

Abbreviations using initials are acceptable in most writing as long as they are familiar to readers. Abbreviations of three or more words are usually written without periods.

INSTITUTIONS	LSU, UCLA, TCU
ORGANIZATIONS	CIA, FBI, YMCA, AFL-CIO
CORPORATIONS	IBM, CBS, ITT
PEOPLE	JFK, LBJ, FDR
COUNTRIES	U.S.A. (or USA)

NOTE: If a name or term (such as *operation room*) appears often in a piece of writing, then its abbreviation (*O.R.*) can cut down on extra words. Spell out the full term at its first appearance, indicate its abbreviation in parentheses, and then use the abbreviation.

31 *B.C., A.D., A.M., P.M., no.,* and *$*

Use certain abbreviations only with specific dates or numbers.

44 B.C.	11:26 A.M. (*or* a.m.)	no. 36 (*or* No. 36)
A.D. 1492	8:05 P.M. (*or* p.m.)	$7.41

The abbreviation B.C. ("before Christ") always follows a date, whereas A.D. (*anno Domini,* Latin for "year of the Lord") precedes a date.

NOTE: B.C.E. ("before the common era") and C.E. ("common era") are increasingly replacing B.C. and A.D., respectively. Both follow the date.

Latin abbreviations

Generally, use the common Latin abbreviations (without underlining) only in source citations and comments in parentheses.

i.e.	*id est:* that is
cf.	*confer:* compare
e.g.	*exempli gratia:* for example
et al.	*et alii:* and others
etc.	*et cetera:* and so forth
N.B.	*nota bene:* note well

He said he would be gone a fortnight (i.e., two weeks).
Bloom et al., editors, *Anthology of Light Verse*

Words usually spelled out

In most academic, general, and business writing, certain words should always be spelled out. (In technical writing, however, these words are more often abbreviated.)

Units of measurement
The dog is thirty *inches* (not *in.*) high.
It once swam 2 *miles* (not *mi.*) across a lake.

Geographical names
The publisher is in *Massachusetts* (not *Mass.* or *MA*).
It moved from *Canada* (not *Can.*).

Names of days, months, and holidays
The truce was signed on *Tuesday* (not *Tues.*), *April* (not *Apr.*) 16.
It was ratified by *Christmas* (not *Xmas*).

Names of people
Robert (not *Robt.*) Frost writes accessible poems.
Virginia (not *Va.*) Woolf was British.

Courses of instruction
I'm majoring in *political science* (not *poli. sci.*).
Economics (not *Econ.*) is a useful course.

32

NUMBERS

In scientific and technical writing, all numbers are usually written as figures. In business writing, all numbers over ten are usually written as figures. In other academic and general writing—the subject of this chapter—numbers are more often spelled out.

Figures vs. words

Use figures for most numbers that require more than two words to spell out.

> The leap year has *366* days.
> The population of Minot, North Dakota, is about *32,800*.

Spell out numbers of one or two words.

> The ball game drew *forty-two thousand* people. [A hyphenated number may be considered one word.]

NOTE: Use a combination of figures and words for round numbers over a million: *26 million, 2.45 billion.* And use either all figures or all words when several numbers appear together in a passage, even if convention would require a mixture.

Commonly used figures

We conventionally use figures for certain information, even when the numbers could be spelled out in one or two words.

Days and years	Exact amounts of money
June 18, 1985 A.D. 12	
1999 456 B.C.	$3.5 million $4.50

Pages, chapters, volumes, acts, scenes, lines	Decimals, percentages, and fractions
Chapter 9, page 123	22.5 $3\frac{1}{2}$
Hamlet, Act 5, Scene 3	48% (*or* 48 percent)

Addresses	Scores and statistics
355 Clinton Avenue	21 to 7 a ratio of 8 to 1
Washington, D.C. 20036	The time of day
	9:00 3:45

Beginnings of sentences

For clarity, spell out any number that begins a sentence. If the number requires more than two words, reword the sentence so that the number falls later and can be expressed as a figure.

FAULTY	*103* visitors asked for refunds.
AWKWARD	*One hundred three* visitors asked for refunds.
REVISED	Of the visitors, *103* asked for refunds.

32

V

USING AND DOCUMENTING SOURCES

EVALUATION OF SOURCES

The use of sources to form, support, and extend your own ideas requires, first, that you find and evaluate the sources. Your librarian can help you find sources. To evaluate them, scan introductions, tables of contents, and headings. Look for information about authors' backgrounds that will help you understand their expertise and bias. Try to answer the following questions about each source:

• Is the work relevant?

Does the source devote some attention to your topic?
Where in the source are you likely to find relevant information or ideas?
Is the source appropriately specialized for your needs? Check the source's treatment of a topic you know something about, to ensure that it is neither too superficial nor too technical.
How important is the source likely to be for your writing?

• Is the work reliable?

How up to date is the source? If the publication date is not recent, be sure that other sources will give you more current views.
Is the author an expert in the field? Look for an author biography, or look up the author in a biographical reference.
What is the author's bias? Check biographical information or the author's own preface or introduction. Consider what others have written about the author or the source. (To find such commentary, ask your librarian for citation indexes or book review indexes.)
Whatever his or her bias, does the author reason soundly, provide adequate evidence, and consider opposing views?

Don't expect to find harmony among sources, for reasonable people often disagree in their opinions. Thus you must deal honestly with the gaps and conflicts in sources. Old sources, superficial ones, slanted ones—these should be offset in your research and your writing by sources that are newer, more thorough, or more objective.

34

NOTES: SUMMARY, PARAPHRASE, DIRECT QUOTATION

Taking notes from sources is not a mechanical process of copying from books and periodicals. Rather, as you read and take notes you assess and organize the information in your sources. Researchers generally rely on the following techniques.

Summary

When you SUMMARIZE, you condense an extended idea or argument into a sentence or more in your own words. Summary is most useful when you want to record the gist of an author's idea without the background or supporting evidence. Here, for example, is a passage summarized in a sentence.

ORIGINAL

Generalizing about male and female styles of management is a tricky business, because stereotypes have traditionally been used to keep women down. Not too long ago it was a widely accepted truth that women were unstable, indecisive, temperamental and manipulative and weren't good team members because they'd never played football. In fighting off these prejudices many women simply tried to adopt masculine traits in the office. —ANN HUGHEY and ERIC GELMAN, "Managing the Woman's Way," *Newsweek*, page 47

SUMMARY

Rather than be labeled with the sexist stereotypes that prevented their promotions, many women adopted masculine qualities.

Paraphrase

When you PARAPHRASE, you follow much more closely the author's original presentation, but you still restate it in your own words. Paraphrase is most useful when you want to reconstruct an author's line of reasoning but don't feel the original words merit direct quotation. Here is a paraphrase of the passage above by Hughey and Gelman.

PARAPHRASE

Because of the risk of stereotyping, which has served as a tool to block women from management, it is difficult to characterize a feminine management style. Women have been cited for their emotionality, instability, and lack of team spirit, among other qualities. Many women have defended themselves at work by adopting the qualities of men.

(Poor and revised paraphrases appear on p. 85.)

Direct quotation

If your purpose is to analyze a particular work, such as a short story or historical document, then you will use many direct quotations from the work. But otherwise you should quote from sources only in the following circumstances:

- The author's original satisfies one of these requirements:

  The language is unusually vivid, bold, or inventive.
  The quotation cannot be paraphrased without distortion or loss of meaning.
  The words themselves are at issue in your interpretation.
  The quotation represents and emphasizes the view of an important expert.
  The quotation is a graph, diagram, or table.

- The quotation is as short as possible.

  It includes only material relevant to your point.
  It is edited to eliminate examples and other unneeded material. (See below.)

When taking a quotation from a source, copy the material *carefully*. Take down the author's exact wording, spelling, capitalization, and punctuation. Proofread every direct quotation *at least twice*, and be sure you have supplied big quotation marks so that later you won't confuse the direct quotation with a paraphrase or summary. If you want to make changes for clarity, use brackets (see p. 63). If you want to omit irrelevant words or sentences, use ellipsis marks, usually three spaced periods (see p. 62).

35

35
PLAGIARISM

PLAGIARISM (from a Latin word for "kidnapper") is the presentation of someone else's ideas or words as your own. Whether deliberate or accidental, plagiarism is a serious and often punishable offense.

- *Deliberate* plagiarism includes copying a sentence from a source and passing it off as your own, summarizing someone else's ideas without acknowledging your debt, or buying a term paper and handing it in as your own.
- *Accidental* plagiarism includes forgetting to place quotation marks around another writer's words, omitting a source citation because you are not aware of the need for it, or carelessly copying a source when you mean to paraphrase.

What not to acknowledge

Your independent material

You are not required to acknowledge your own observations, thoughts, compilations of facts, or experimental results, expressed in your own words and format.

Common knowledge

You need not acknowledge common knowledge: the standard information of a field of study as well as folk literature and commonsense observations.

If you do not know a subject well enough to determine whether a piece of information is common knowledge, make a record of the source. As you read more about the subject, the information may come up repeatedly without acknowledgment, in which case it is probably common knowledge. But if you are still in doubt when you finish your research, always acknowledge the source.

What to acknowledge

You must always acknowledge other people's independent material—that is, any facts or ideas that are not common knowledge or your own. The source may be anything, including a book, an article, a movie, an interview, a microfilmed document, or a computer program. You must acknowledge not only ideas or facts themselves but also the language and format in which the ideas or facts appear, if you use them. That is, the wording, sentence structures, arrangement of ideas, and special graphics (such as a diagram) created by another writer belong to that writer just as his or her ideas do.

How to avoid plagiarism

The following example baldly plagiarizes both the structure and the words of the original quotation from Jessica Mitford's *Kind and Usual Punishment,* page 9.

ORIGINAL   The character and mentality of the keepers may be of more importance in understanding prisons than the character and mentality of the kept.

PLAGIARISM   But the character of prison officials (the keepers) is more important in understanding prisons than the character of prisoners (the kept).

The next example is more subtle plagiarism, because it changes Mitford's sentence structure. But it still uses her words.

PLAGIARISM   In understanding prisons, we should know more about the character and mentality of the keepers than of the kept.

The plagiarism in these examples can be remedied by placing Mitford's exact words in quotation marks, changing her sentence structure when not quoting, and citing the source properly (here, in MLA style).

REVISION
(QUOTATION)   According to one critic of the penal system, "The character and mentality of the keepers may be of more importance in understanding prisons than the character and mentality of the kept" (Mitford 9).

REVISION
(PARAPHRASE)   One critic of the penal system maintains that we may be able to learn more about prisons from the psychology of the prison officials than from that of the prisoners (Mitford 9).

The following checklist can help you avoid plagiarism.

• What type of source are you using: your own independent material, common knowledge, or someone else's independent material? You must acknowledge someone else's material.
• If you are quoting someone else's material, is the quotation exact? Have you inserted quotation marks around quotations run into the text? Have you shown omissions with ellipsis marks and additions with brackets?
• If you are paraphrasing or summarizing someone else's

material, have you used your own words and sentence structures? Does your paraphrase or summary employ quotation marks when you resort to the author's exact language? Have you represented the author's meaning without distortion?

• Is each use of someone else's material acknowledged in your text? Are all your source citations complete and accurate?

• Does your list of works cited include all the sources you have drawn from in writing your paper?

36

INTRODUCTION OF
BORROWED MATERIAL

When using summaries, paraphrases, and quotations, integrate them smoothly into your own sentences. In the passage below, the writer initially did not mesh the structures of her own and her source's sentences.

| AWKWARD | One editor disagrees with this view and "a good reporter does not fail to separate opinions from facts" (Lyman 52). |
| REVISED | One editor disagrees with this view, maintaining that "a good reporter does not fail to separate opinions from facts" (Lyman 52). |

Even when not conflicting with your own sentence structure, borrowed material will be ineffective if you merely dump it in readers' laps without explaining how you intend it to be understood.

| DUMPED | Many news editors and reporters maintain that it is impossible to keep personal opinions from influencing the selection and presentation of facts. "True, news reporters, like everyone else, form impressions of what they see and hear. However, a good reporter does not fail to separate opinions from facts" (Lyman 52). |
| REVISED | Many news editors and reporters maintain that it is impossible to keep personal opinions from influencing the selection and presentation of facts. Yet not all authorities agree with this |

view. One editor grants that "news reporters, like everyone else, form impressions of what they see and hear." But, he insists, "a good reporter does not fail to separate opinions from facts" (Lyman 52).

You can add other information to integrate a quotation and inform readers why you are using it.

AUTHOR
NAMED

... Harold Lyman grants that "news reporters, like everyone else, form impressions of what they see and hear." But, Lyman insists, "a good reporter does not fail to separate opinions from facts" (52).

TITLE
GIVEN

... Harold Lyman, in his book *The Conscience of the Journalist,* grants that "news reporters, like everyone else, form impressions of what they see and hear." But, Lyman insists, "a good reporter does not fail to separate opinions from facts" (52).

CREDENTIALS
GIVEN

... Harold Lyman, a newspaper editor for more than forty years, grants that "news reporters, like everyone else, form impressions of what they see and hear." But, Lyman insists, "a good reporter does not fail to separate opinions from facts" (52).

You need not name the author, source, or credentials in your text when you are simply establishing facts or weaving together facts and opinions from varied sources (although, of course, you must still acknowledge each source in a citation).

See pages 66–67 for when to run quotations into your own text and when to display them separately from your text.

37

DOCUMENTATION OF SOURCES: MLA STYLE

Every time you borrow the words, facts, or ideas of others, you must DOCUMENT the source—that is, supply a reference (or document) telling readers that you borrowed the material and where you borrowed it from.

Editors and teachers in most academic disciplines require special documentation formats (or styles) in their scholarly journals and in students' papers. This chapter concentrates on a style of in-text citation widely used in the arts and humanities: that of the Modern Language Association, published in the *MLA Handbook for Writers of Research Papers*, 3rd ed. (1988). The next two chapters present a style widely used in the social sciences, that of the American Psychological Association (APA), and a system of footnotes or endnotes. Beyond this book several guides outline other documentation styles:

American Anthropological Association. "Style Guide and Information for Authors." *American Anthropologist* (1977): 774-79.

American Chemical Society. *Handbook for Authors of Papers in American Chemical Society Publications*. 1978.

American Institute of Physics. *Style Manual for Guidance in the Preparation of Papers*. 3rd ed. 1978.

American Mathematical Society. *A Manual for Authors of Mathematical Papers*. 8th ed. 1980.

American Medical Association. *Style Book: Editorial Manual*. 6th ed. 1976.

American Sociological Association. "Editorial Guidelines." Inside front cover of each issue of *American Sociological Review*.

The Chicago Manual of Style. 13th ed. 1982.

Council of Biology Editors. *CBE Style Manual: A Guide for Authors, Editors, and Publishers in the Biological Sciences*. 5th ed. 1983.

Turabian, Kate L. *A Manual for Writers of Term Papers, Theses, and Dissertations*. 5th ed. Rev. and exp. Bonnie Birtwistle Honigsblum. 1987.

Ask your instructor which style he or she prefers.

MLA parenthetical citations

The documentation system of the *MLA Handbook* employs brief parenthetical citations within the text that direct readers to the list of works cited at the end of the text.

Citation formats

The in-text citations of sources must include just enough information for the reader to locate (1) the appropriate source in your list of works cited and (2) the place in the source where the borrowed material appears. Usually, you can meet

Index to MLA parenthetical citations

both these requirements by providing the author's last name and the page(s) in the source on which the borrowed material appears.

1. AUTHOR NOT NAMED IN THE TEXT

One researcher concludes that "women impose a distinctive construction on moral problems, seeing moral dilemmas in terms of conflicting responsibilities" (Gilligan 105).

2. AUTHOR NAMED IN THE TEXT

One researcher, Carol Gilligan, concludes that "women impose a distinctive construction on moral problems, seeing moral dilemmas in terms of conflicting responsibilities" (105).

3. A WORK WITH TWO OR THREE AUTHORS

As Frieden and Sagalyn observe, "The poor and the minorities were the leading victims of highway and renewal programs" (29).

4. A WORK WITH MORE THAN THREE AUTHORS

It took the combined forces of the Americans, Europeans, and Japanese to break the rebel siege of Beijing in 1900 (Lopez et al. 362).

5. AN ENTIRE WORK (NO PAGE NUMBERS)

Boyd deals with the need to acknowledge and come to terms with our fear of nuclear technology.

6. A MULTIVOLUME WORK

After issuing the Emancipation Proclamation, Lincoln said, "What I did, I did after very full deliberations, and under a very heavy and solemn sense of responsibility" (5: 438).

7. A WORK BY AN AUTHOR OF TWO OR MORE CITED WORKS

At about age seven, most children begin to use appropriate gestures to reinforce their stories (Gardner, Arts 144-45).

8. AN UNSIGNED WORK

One article notes that a death-row inmate may demand his own execution to achive a fleeting notoriety ("Right").

9. A GOVERNMENT DOCUMENT OR A WORK WITH A CORPORATE AUTHOR

A 1983 report by the Hawaii Department of Education predicts a slow increase in enrollments (6).

10. A SOURCE REFERRED TO BY ANOTHER SOURCE

George Davino maintains that "even small children have vivid ideas about nuclear energy" (qtd. in Boyd 22).

11. A LITERARY WORK

```
Toward the end of James's novel, Maggie suddenly
feels "the intimate, the immediate, the familiar,
as she hadn't had them for so long" (535; pt. 6,
ch. 41).
```

```
Later in King Lear Shakespeare has the disguised
Edgar say, "The prince of darkness is a gentle-
man" (3.4.147).
```

The citation above lists act number, scene number, and line number, respectively.

12. MORE THAN ONE WORK

```
Two recent articles point out that a computer
badly used can be less efficient than no computer
at all (Richards 162; Gough and Hall 201).
```

Footnotes or endnotes in special circumstances

Footnotes or endnotes may supplement parenthetical citations when you cite several sources at once, when you comment on a source, or when you provide information that does not fit easily in the text. Signal a footnote or endnote in your text with a numeral raised above the appropriate line. Then write a note with the same numeral.

TEXT ```At least five subsequent studies have
       confirmed these results.```[1]

NOTE   [1] ```Abbott and Winger 266-68; Casner
       27; Hoyenga 78-79; Marino 36; Tripp,
       Tripp, and Walk 179-83.```

If the note appears as a footnote, place it at the bottom of the page on which the citation appears, set it off from the text with quadruple spacing, and single-space the note itself. If the note appears as an endnote, place it in numerical order with the other endnotes on a page between the text and the list of works cited; double-space all the endnotes.

MLA list of works cited

At the end of your paper, a list titled "Works Cited" includes all the sources you quoted, paraphrased, or summarized in your paper. For this list, arrange your sources in alphabetical order by the last name of the author. If an author is not given in the source, alphabetize the source by the first main word of the title (excluding *A*, *An*, or *The*). In the models that follow for various sources, note these main features:

• Double-space all entries. Type the first line of each entry at the left margin, and indent all subsequent lines five spaces.
• List the author's name last-name first. If there are two or three authors, list all names after the first in normal order. Separate the names with commas.
• Give full titles, capitalizing all important words (see p. 73). (For periodical titles, omit any *A*, *An*, or *The*.) Underline

---

Index to MLA works-cited models

37

the titles of books and periodicals; place titles of periodical articles in quotation marks.

- Provide publication information after the title, such as place of publication, publisher's name, and date (for books) and the volume or issue number, date, and page numbers (for articles).
- Separate the main parts of an entry with periods followed by two spaces.

Books

1. A BOOK WITH ONE AUTHOR

```
Gilligan, Carol.  In a Different Voice: Psycho-

    logical Theory and Women's Development.

    Cambridge: Harvard UP, 1982.
```

37

2. A BOOK WITH TWO OR THREE AUTHORS

Frieden, Bernard J., and Lynne B. Sagalyn. Downtown, Inc.: How America Rebuilds Cities.
Cambridge: MIT, 1989

3. A BOOK WITH MORE THAN THREE AUTHORS

Lopez, Robert S., et al. Civilizations: Western
and World. Boston: Little, 1975.

4. TWO OR MORE WORKS BY THE SAME AUTHOR(S)

Gardner, Howard. The Arts and Human Development.
New York: Wiley, 1973.

---. The Quest for Mind: Piaget, Lévi-Strauss,
and the Structuralist Movement. New York:
Knopf, 1973.

5. A BOOK WITH AN EDITOR

Ruitenbeek, Hendrick, ed. Freud as We Knew Him.
Detroit: Wayne State UP, 1973.

6. A BOOK WITH AN AUTHOR AND AN EDITOR

Melville, Herman. The Confidence Man: His Masquerade. Ed. Hershel Parker. New York:
Norton, 1971.

7. A TRANSLATION

Alighieri, Dante. The Inferno. Trans. John
Ciardi. New York: NAL, 1971.

8. A BOOK WITH A CORPORATE AUTHOR

Lorenz, Inc. Research in Social Studies Teach-
ing. Baltimore: Arrow, 1992.

9. AN ANONYMOUS BOOK

Webster's Ninth New Collegiate Dictionary.

    Springfield: Merriam, 1987.

10. A LATER EDITION

Bollinger, Dwight L. Aspects of Language. 2nd

    ed. New York: Harcourt, 1975.

11. A BOOK WITH A TITLE IN ITS TITLE

Eco, Umberto. Postscript to The Name of the

    Rose. Trans. William Weaver. New York:

    Harcourt, 1983.

12. A WORK IN MORE THAN ONE VOLUME

Lincoln, Abraham. The Collected Works of Abraham

    Lincoln. Ed. Roy P. Basler. 8 vols. New

    Brunswick: Rutgers UP, 1953.

Lincoln, Abraham. The Collected Works of Abraham

    Lincoln. Ed. Roy P. Basler. Vol. 5. New

    Brunswick: Rutgers UP, 1953. 8 vols.

13. A WORK IN A SERIES

Bergman, Ingmar. The Seventh Seal. Modern Film

    Scripts Series. New York: Simon, 1968.

14. A SELECTION FROM AN ANTHOLOGY OR COLLECTION

Auden, W. H. "A Healthy Spot." The Collected

    Poetry of W. H. Auden. New York: Random,

    1945. 134.

15. TWO OR MORE SELECTIONS FROM THE SAME ANTHOLOGY

Brooks, Rosetta. "Streetwise." Martin 38–39.

Martin, Richard, ed. The New Urban Landscape.

    New York: Rizzoli, 1990.

37

Plotkin, Mark J. "Tropical Forests and the Urban
Landscape." Martin 50-51.

16. AN INTRODUCTION, PREFACE, FOREWORD, OR AFTERWORD

Donaldson, Norman. Introduction. The Claver-
ings. By Anthony Trollope. New York: Dover, 1977. vii-xv.

17. AN ENCYCLOPEDIA OR ALMANAC

"Mammoth." The New Columbia Encyclopedia. 1975.

Mark, Herman F. "Polymers." Encyclopaedia Bri-
tannica: Macropaedia. 1974.

Periodicals: Journals, magazines, newspapers

18. A SIGNED ARTICLE IN A JOURNAL WITH CONTINUOUS PAGINATION THROUGHOUT THE ANNUAL VOLUME

Lever, Janet. "Sex Differences in the Games
Children Play." Social Problems 23 (1976):
478-87.

19. A SIGNED ARTICLE IN A JOURNAL THAT PAGES ISSUES SEPARATELY OR NUMBERS ONLY ISSUES, NOT VOLUMES

Boyd, Sarah. "Nuclear Terror." Adaptation to
Change 7.4 (1981): 20-23.

20. A SIGNED ARTICLE IN A MONTHLY OR BIMONTHLY MAGAZINE

Stein, Harry. "Living with Lies." Esquire Dec.
1981: 23.

21. A SIGNED ARTICLE IN A WEEKLY OR BIWEEKLY MAGAZINE

Stevens, Mark. "Low and Behold." New Republic
24 Dec. 1990: 27-33.

22. A SIGNED ARTICLE IN A DAILY NEWSPAPER

Nieves, Evelyn. "How to Shoot Baseball." New
    York Times 18 June 1993: B5.

23. AN UNSIGNED ARTICLE

"The Right to Die." Time 11 Oct. 1976: 101.

24. AN EDITORIAL OR LETTER TO THE EDITOR

"Bodily Intrusions." Editorial. New York Times
    29 Aug. 1990: A20.

Dowding, Michael. Letter. Economist 5-11 Jan.
    1985: 4.

25. A REVIEW

Dunne, John Gregory. "The Secret of Danny Santi-
    ago." Rev. of Famous All over Town, by
    Danny Santiago. New York Review of Books 16
    Aug. 1984: 17-27.

26. AN ABSTRACT OF A DISSERTATION

Steciw, Steven K. "Alterations to the Pessac
    Project of Le Corbusier." DAI 46 (1986):
    565C. Cambridge U, England.

Other sources

27. A GOVERNMENT DOCUMENT

United States. Cong. House. Committee on Ways
    and Means. Medicare Payment for Outpatient
    Physical and Occupational Therapy Services.
    102nd Cong., 1st sess. Washington: GPO,
    1991.

37

Mozart, Wolfgang Amadeus. Piano Concerto no. 20
     in D Minor, K. 466.

Sargent, John Singer. <u>Venetian Doorway</u>. Metro-
     politan Museum of Art, New York.

Allen, Woody, dir. <u>Manhattan</u>. With Allen, Diane
     Keaton, Michael Murphy, Meryl Streep, and
     Anne Byrne. United Artists, 1979.

<u>Serenade</u>. Videotape. Chor. George Balanchine.
     With San Francisco Ballet. Dir. Hilary
     Beane. San Francisco Ballet, 1987. 24 min.

<u>King of America</u>. Writ. B. J. Merholz. Music
     Elizabeth Swados. With Larry Atlas, Andreas
     Katsulas, Barry Miller, and Michael Walden.
     American Playhouse. PBS. WNET, New York.
     19 Jan. 1982.

<u>The English Only Restaurant</u>. By Silvio Martinez
     Palau. Dir. Susana Tubert. Puerto Rico
     Traveling Theater, New York. 27 July 1990.

Ozawa, Seiji, cond. Boston Symphony Orch. Con-
     cert. Symphony Hall, Boston. 25 Apr. 1991.

Mitchell, Joni. <u>For the Roses</u>. Asylum, SD-5057,
     1972.

37

Brahms, Johannes. Concerto no. 2 in B-flat, op.
     83. Perf. Artur Rubinstein. Cond. Eugene
     Ormandy. Philadelphia Orch. RCA, RK-1243,
     1972.

33. A LETTER

Buttolph, Mrs. Laura E. Letter to Rev. and Mrs.
     C. C. Jones. 20 June 1857. In The Children
     of Pride: A True Story of Georgia and the
     Civil War. Ed. Robert Manson Myers. New
     Haven: Yale UP, 1972. 334.
Packer, Ann E. Letter to the author. 15 June
     1988.

34. A LECTURE OR ADDRESS

Carlone, Dennis J. "Urban Design in the 1990s."
     Sixth Symposium on Urban Issues. City of
     Cambridge. Cambridge, 16 Oct. 1988.

35. AN INTERVIEW

Graaf, Vera. Personal interview. 19 Dec. 1990.
Martin, William. Interview. "Give Me That Big
     Time Religion." Frontline. PBS. WGBH,
     Boston. 13 Feb. 1984.

36. AN INFORMATION OR COMPUTER SERVICE

Jolson, Maria K. Music Education for Preschool-
     ers. ERIC, 1981. ED 264 488.
Palfry, Andrew. "Choice of Mates in Identical
     Twins." Modern Psychology Jan. 1979: 16-27.
     DIALOG file 261, item 5206341.

37

37. COMPUTER SOFTWARE

<u>Project Scheduler 6000.</u> Computer software. Sci-

tor, 1991. MS-DOS, 256 KB, disk.

38

DOCUMENTATION OF SOURCES: APA STYLE

The documentation style of the American Psychological Association is used in psychology and some other social sciences and is very similar to the styles in sociology, economics, and other disciplines. The following adapts the APA style from the *Publication Manual of the American Psychological Association,* 3rd ed. (1983).

APA parenthetical citations

In the APA style, parenthetical citations in the text refer to a list of sources at the end of the text. The basic parenthetical citation contains the author's last name, the date of publication, and often the page number from which material is borrowed.

1. AUTHOR NOT NAMED IN THE TEXT

One critic of Milgram's experiments insisted that

Index to APA parenthetical citations

the subjects should have been fully informed of
the possible effects on them (Baumrind, 1968, p.
34).

2. AUTHOR NAMED IN THE TEXT

Baumrind (1968, p. 34) insisted that the subjects
in Milgram's study should have been fully informed of the possible effects on them.

3. A WORK WITH TWO AUTHORS

Pepinsky and DeStefano (1977) demonstrate that a
teacher's language often reveals hidden biases.

One study (Pepinsky & DeStefano, 1977) demon-
strates hidden biases in teachers' language.

4. A WORK WITH THREE TO SIX AUTHORS

First reference:

Pepinsky, Dunn, Rentl, and Corson (1973) further
demonstrate the biases evident in gestures.

Later references:

In the work of Pepinsky et al. (1973), the loaded
gestures include head shakes and eye contact.

5. A WORK WITH MORE THAN SIX AUTHORS

One study (Rutter et al., 1976) attempts to explain these geographical differences in adoles-
cent experience.

6. A WORK WITH A CORPORATE AUTHOR

An earlier prediction was even more somber (Lorenz, Inc., 1970).

38

7. AN ANONYMOUS WORK

One article ("Right to Die," 1976) noted that a
death-row inmate may crave notoriety.

8. A WORK BY AN AUTHOR OF TWO OR MORE CITED WORKS

At about age seven, most children begin to use
appropriate gestures to reinforce their stories
(Gardner, 1973a, pp. 144-145).

(See the reference for this source, p. 104.)

9. TWO OR MORE WORKS BY DIFFERENT AUTHORS

Two studies (Herskowitz, 1974; Marconi & Hamblen,
1980) found that periodic safety instruction can
dramatically reduce employees' accidents.

10. A SOURCE REFERRED TO BY ANOTHER SOURCE

Supporting data appear in a study by Wong (cited
in Marconi & Hamblen, 1980).

38

APA reference list

In APA style, the in-text parenthetical citations refer to the
list of sources at the end of the text. This list, titled "References," includes full publication information on every source
cited in the paper. The sources are arranged alphabetically by
the author's last name or, if there is no author, by the first
main word of the title. In the models that follow for various
sources, observe these features:

• Double-space all entries. Type the first line of each entry at
  the left magin, and indent all subsequent lines three spaces.
• List all authors last-name first, separating names and parts
  of names with commas. Use initials for first and middle
  names. Use an ampersand (&) rather than "and" before the
  last author's name.
• In titles of books and articles, capitalize only the first word
  of the title, the first word of the subtitle, and proper names;
  all other words begin with small letters. In titles of journals,

capitalize all significant words. Underline the titles of books and journals. Do not underline or use quotation marks around the titles of articles.

- Give full names of publishers, excluding "Co.," "Inc.," and the like.
- Use the abbreviation "p." or "pp." before page numbers in books, magazines, and newspapers, but *not* for scholarly journals. For inclusive page numbers, include all figures: "667–668."
- Separate the parts of the reference (author, date, title, and publication information) with a period and two spaces.

Index to APA references

38

Books

1. A BOOK WITH ONE AUTHOR

Rodriguez, R. (1982). <u>A hunger of memory: The education of Richard Rodriguez</u>. Boston: David R. Godine.

2. A BOOK WITH TWO OR MORE AUTHORS

Nesselroade, J. R., & Baltes, P. B. (1979). <u>Longitudinal research in the study of behavioral development</u>. New York: Academic Press.

3. A BOOK WITH AN EDITOR

Dohrenwend, B. S., & Dohrenwend, B. P. (Eds.). (1974). <u>Stressful life events: Their nature and effects</u>. New York: John Wiley.

4. A BOOK WITH A TRANSLATOR

Trajan, P. D. (1927). <u>Psychology of animals</u>. (H. Simone, Trans.). Washington, DC: Halperin & Bros.

5. A BOOK WITH A CORPORATE AUTHOR

Lorenz, Inc. (1992). <u>Research in social studies teaching</u>. Baltimore: Arrow Books.

6. AN ANONYMOUS BOOK

<u>Webster's seventh new collegiate dictionary</u>. (1963). Springfield: G. & C. Merriam.

7. TWO OR MORE WORKS BY THE SAME AUTHOR(S)

Gardner, H. (1973a). <u>The arts and human development</u>. New York: John Wiley.

38

Gardner, H. (1973b). The quest for mind: Piaget, Lévi-Strauss, and the structuralist movement. New York: Alfred A. Knopf.

8. A LATER EDITION

Bollinger, D. L. (1975). Aspects of language
(2nd ed.). New York: Harcourt Brace Jovano-
vich.

9. A WORK IN MORE THAN ONE VOLUME

Lincoln, A. (1953). The collected works of
Abraham Lincoln (R. P. Basler, Ed.). (Vol.
5). New Brunswick: Rutgers University Press.

Lincoln, A. (1953). The collected works of
Abraham Lincoln (R. P. Basler, Ed.). (Vols.
1-8). New Brunswick: Rutgers University Press.

10. AN ARTICLE OR CHAPTER IN AN EDITED BOOK

Paykel, E. S. (1974). Life stress and psychiat-
ric disorder: Applications of the clinical ap-
proach. In B. S. Dohrenwend & B. P. Dohrenwend (Eds.), Stressful life events: Their
nature and effects (pp. 239-264). New York:
John Wiley.

Periodicals: Journals, magazines, newspapers

**11. AN ARTICLE IN A JOURNAL WITH CONTINUOUS PAGINATION
THROUGHOUT THE ANNUAL VOLUME**

Emery, R. E. (1982). Marital turmoil: Interper-
sonal conflict and the children of discord and
divorce. Psychological Bulletin, 92, 310-330.

38

12. AN ARTICLE IN A JOURNAL THAT PAGES ISSUES SEPARATELY

Boyd, S. (1981). Nuclear terror. Adaptation to
    Change, 7(4), 20-23.

13. AN ARTICLE IN A MAGAZINE

Van Gelder, L. (1986, December). Countdown to
    motherhood: When should you have a baby? Ms.,
    pp. 37-39, 74.

14. AN ARTICLE IN A NEWSPAPER

Herbers, J. (1988, March 6). A different Dixie:
    Few but sturdy threads tie new South to old.
    The New York Times, sec. 4, p. 1.

15. AN UNSIGNED ARTICLE

The right to die. (1976, October 11). Time, p.
    101.

16. A REVIEW

Dinnage, R. (1987, November 29). Against the
    master and his men. [Review of A mind of her
    own: The life of Karen Horney.] The New York
    Times Book Review, pp. 10-11.

Other sources

17. A REPORT

Gerald, K. (1958). Micro-moral problems in ob-
    stetric care (Report No. NP-71). St. Louis:
    Catholic Hospital Association.

18. AN INFORMATION SERVICE

Jolson, Maria K. (1981). Music education for

<u>preschoolers</u>. New York: Teachers College, Co-

lumbia University. (ERIC Document Reproduc-

tion Service No. ED 264 488)

19. A GOVERNMENT DOCUMENT

United States Commission on Civil Rights.

(1983). <u>Greater Baltimore commitment</u>. Wash-

ington DC: Author.

20. AN INTERVIEW

William C. Brisick. (1988, July 1). [Interview

with Ishmael Reed]. <u>Publishers Weekly</u>, pp.

41-42.

21. A VIDEOTAPE OR OTHER NONPRINT SOURCE

Heeley, D. (Director), & Kramer, J. (Producer).

(1988). <u>Bacall on Bogart</u> [Videotape]. New

York: WNET Films.

22. COMPUTER SOFTWARE

<u>Project scheduler 6000</u>. (1991). [Computer pro-

gram]. Orlando: Scitor.

39

39

DOCUMENTATION OF SOURCES: FOOTNOTES OR ENDNOTES

Several disciplines in the arts and humanities use a system of footnotes or endnotes to cite sources. With this system you place a raised numeral ([1]) in the text at the end of the material you are acknowledging, and you number citations consecutively throughout the paper. The notes themselves then fall in the same order, either at the bottoms of the appropriate pages or on separate pages at the end of the paper. Your instructor may request an alphabetical list of sources in addition to notes;

if so, follow the guidelines on pages 92–100 for a list of works cited and place the list at the end of the paper, after any endnotes.

Here are samples of a text reference and a note:

TEXT   While sex-role stereotyping might not be as

obvious as it was in a 1972 study,[7] it re-

mains pervasive in our society.

Index to note models

39

NOTE [7] I. K. Broverman et al., "Sex-Role

Stereotypes: A Current Appraisal," Journal

of Social Issues 28.2 (1972): 59-78.

The format for typing footnotes or endnotes is described on page 91.

The following note models, based on the *MLA Handbook for Writers of Research Papers,* resemble most styles of footnotes or endnotes. These models are for the first reference to a source; for subsequent references, use a shortened note as discussed on pp. 112–13.

Books

1. A BOOK WITH ONE AUTHOR

[1] Carol Gilligan, In a Different Voice: Psy-

chological Theory and Women's Development (Cam-

bridge: Harvard UP, 1982) 27.

2. A BOOK WITH TWO OR THREE AUTHORS

[2] Bernard J. Frieden and Lynne B. Sagalyn,

Downtown, Inc.: How America Rebuilds Cities (Cam-

bridge: MIT, 1989) 16.

3. A BOOK WITH MORE THAN THREE AUTHORS

[3] Robert S. Lopez et al., Civilizations:

Western and World (Boston: Little, 1975) 281-82.

4. A BOOK WITH AN EDITOR

[4] Hendrick Ruitenbeek, ed., Freud as We Knew

Him (Detroit: Wayne State UP, 1973) 64.

5. A BOOK WITH AN AUTHOR AND AN EDITOR

[5] Herman Melville, The Confidence Man: His

Masquerade, ed. Hershel Parker (New York: Norton,

1971) 49.

39

6. A TRANSLATION

⁶ Dante Alighieri, <u>The Inferno</u>, trans. John Ciardi (New York: NAL, 1971) 73-74.

7. AN ANONYMOUS BOOK

⁷ <u>Webster's Ninth New Collegiate Dictionary</u> (Springfield: Merriam, 1987).

8. A LATER EDITION

⁸ Dwight L. Bollinger, <u>Aspects of Language</u>, 2nd ed. (New York: Harcourt, 1975) 20.

9. A WORK IN MORE THAN ONE VOLUME

⁹ Abraham Lincoln, <u>The Collected Works of Abraham Lincoln</u>, ed. Roy P. Basler, 8 vols. (New Brunswick: Rutgers UP, 1953) 5: 426-28.

10. A SELECTION FROM AN ANTHOLOGY

¹⁰ W. H. Auden, "A Healthy Spot," <u>The Collected Poetry of W. H. Auden</u> (New York: Random, 1945) 134.

11. AN ENCYCLOPEDIA

¹¹ "Mammoth," <u>The New Columbia Encyclopedia</u>, 1975.

Periodicals: Journals, magazines, newspapers

12. A SIGNED ARTICLE IN A JOURNAL WITH CONTINUOUS PAGINATION THROUGHOUT THE ANNUAL VOLUME

¹² Janet Lever, "Sex Differences in the Games Children Play," <u>Social Problems</u> 23 (1976): 482.

13. A SIGNED ARTICLE IN A JOURNAL THAT PAGES ISSUES SEPARATELY OR NUMBERS ONLY ISSUES, NOT VOLUMES

[13] Sarah Boyd, "Nuclear Terror," Adaptation to Change 7.4 (1981): 20-21.

14. A SIGNED ARTICLE IN A MAGAZINE OR NEWSPAPER

[14] Mark Stevens, "Low and Behold," New Republic 24 Dec. 1990: 28.

15. AN UNSIGNED ARTICLE

[15] "The Right to Die," Time 11 Oct. 1976: 101.

16. A REVIEW

[16] John Gregory Dunne, "The Secret of Danny Santiago," rev. of Famous All over Town, by Danny Santiago, New York Review of Books 16 Aug. 1984: 20.

17. AN ABSTRACT OF A DISSERTATION

[17] Steven K. Steciw, "Alterations to the Pessac Project of Le Corbusier," DAI 46 (1986): 565C (Cambridge U, England).

Other sources

18. A GOVERNMENT DOCUMENT

[18] United States, Cong., House, Committee on Ways and Means, Medicare Payment for Outpatient Physical and Occupational Therapy Services, 102nd Cong., 1st sess. (Washington: GPO, 1991) 3.

19. A PERFORMANCE (LIVE, RECORDED, BROADCAST)

[19] The English Only Restaurant, by Silvio

Martinez Palau, dir. Susana Tubert, Puerto Rico
Traveling Theater, New York, 27 July 1990.

[19] Johannes Brahms, Concerto no. 2 in
B-flat, op. 83, perf. Artur Rubinstein, cond. Eu-
gene Ormandy, Philadelphia Orch., RCA, RK-1243,
1972.

20. AN INTERVIEW

[20] Vera Graaf, personal interview, 19 Dec.
1990.

21. AN INFORMATION OR COMPUTER SERVICE

[21] Maria K. Jolson, Music Education for Pre-
schoolers (ERIC, 1981) 16 (ED 264 488).

22. COMPUTER SOFTWARE

[22] Project Scheduler 6000, computer software, Scitor, 1991, MS-DOS, 256 KB, disk.

Subsequent references to the same source

Use a shortened citation for subsequent references to a
source you have already cited fully. When you refer to only
one source by the author cited, the *MLA Handbook* recom-
mends that subsequent references carry only the author's
name and the page reference appropriate for the later citation.

[5] Herman Melville, The Confidence Man: His
Masquerade, ed. Hershel Parker (New York: Norton,
1971) 49.

[23] Melville 62.

However, if two of your sources are by the same author,
give a shortened form of the appropriate title so there can be
no confusion about which work you are citing. For example:

[1] Carol Gilligan, In a Different Voice: Psy-

chological Theory and Women's Development (Cam-

bridge: Harvard UP, 1982) 27.

   24 Carol Gilligan, "Moral Development in the

College Years," The Modern American College, ed.

A. Chickering (San Franciso: Jossey-Bass, 1981)

286.

   25 Gilligan, "Moral" 288.

NOTE: The *MLA Handbook* and many other style guides discourage use of the Latin abbreviation "ibid." ("in the same place") as a means of indicating that a citation refers to the source in the preceding note.

39

GLOSSARY OF USAGE

This glossary provides notes on words or phrases that often cause problems for writers. The recommendations for standard written English are based on current dictionaries and usage guides. Items labeled NONSTANDARD should be avoided in speech and especially in writing. Those labeled COLLOQUIAL and SLANG occur in speech and in some informal writing but are best avoided in more formal academic and career writing. (Words and phrases labeled *colloquial* include those labeled by many dictionaries with the equivalent term *informal*.)

a, an Use *a* before words beginning with consonant sounds: *a historian, a one-o'clock class, a university*. Use *an* before words that begin with vowel sounds, including silent *h*'s: *an orgy, an L, an honor.*

The article before an abbreviation depends on how the abbreviation is read: *She was once an AEC aide* (*AEC* is read as three separate letters); *Many Americans opposed a SALT treaty* (*SALT* is read as one word, *salt*).

See also pp. 40–41 on the uses of *a/an* versus *the.*

accept, except *Accept* is a verb° meaning "receive." *Except* is usually a preposition° or conjunction° meaning "but for" or "other than"; when it is used as a verb, it means "leave out." *I can accept all your suggestions except the last one. I'm sorry you excepted my last suggestion from your list.*

advice, advise *Advice* is a noun,° and *advise* is a verb:° *Take my advice; do as I advise you.*

affect, effect Usually *affect* is a verb,° meaning "to influence," and *effect* is a noun, meaning "result": *The drug did not affect his driving; in fact, it seemed to have no effect at all*. But *effect* occasionally is used as a verb meaning "to bring about": *Her efforts effected a change*. And *affect* is used in psychology as a noun meaning "feeling or emotion": *One can infer much about affect from behavior.*

all ready, already *All ready* means "completely prepared," and *already* means "by now" or "before now": *We were all ready to go to the movie, but it had already started.*

all right *All right* is always two words. *Alright* is a common misspelling.

114

all together, altogether   *All together* means "in unison," or "gathered in one place." *Altogether* means "entirely." *It's not altogether true that our family never spends vacations all together.*

allusion, illusion   An *allusion* is an indirect reference, and an *illusion* is a deceptive appearance: *Paul's constant allusions to Shakespeare created the illusion that he was an intellectual.*

a lot   *A lot* is always two words, used informally to mean "many." *Alot* is a common misspelling.

among, between   In general, use *between* only for relationships of two and *among* for more than two.

amount, number   *Amount* refers to a quantity of something (a singular noun) that cannot be counted. *Number* refers to countable items (a plural noun). *The amount of tax depends on the number of deductions.*

and/or   *And/or* indicates three options: one or the other or both (*The decision is made by the mayor and/or the council*). If you mean all three options, *and/or* is appropriate. Otherwise, use *and* if you mean both, *or* if you mean either.

anxious, eager   *Anxious* means "nervous" or "worried" and is usually followed by *about*. *Eager* means "looking forward" and is usually followed by *to*. *I've been anxious about getting blisters. I'm eager (not anxious) to get new cross-training shoes.*

anybody, any body; anyone, any one   *Anybody* and *anyone* are indefinite pronouns;° *any body* is a noun° modified by *any; any one* is a pronoun° or adjective° modified by *any. How can anybody communicate with any body of government? Can anyone help Amy? She has more work than any one person can handle.*

any more, anymore   *Anymore* means "no more"; *anymore* means "now." Both are used in negative constructions: *He doesn't want any more. She doesn't live here anymore.*

anyways, anywheres   Nonstandard for *anyway* and *anywhere*.

are, is   Use *are* with a plural subject° (*books are*), *is* with a singular subject (*book is*). See pp. 25–27.

as   Substituting for *because, since,* or *while, as* may be vague or ambiguous: *As we were stopping to rest, we decided to eat lunch.*

(Does *as* mean "while" or "because"?) *As* never should be used as a substitute for *whether* or *who*. *I'm not sure whether* (not *as*) *we can make it. That's the man who* (not *as*) *gave me directions.*

as, like   In formal speech and writing, *like* should not introduce a full clause.° The preferred choice is *as* or *as if: The plan succeeded as* (not *like*) *we hoped.* Use *like* only before a word or phrase: *Other plans like it have failed.*

at this point in time   Wordy for *now, at this point,* or *at this time.*

awful, awfully   Strictly speaking, *awful* means "awe-inspiring." As intensifiers meaning "very" or "extremely" (*He tried awfully hard*), *awful* and *awfully* should be avoided in formal speech or writing.

a while, awhile   *Awhile* is an adverb;° *a while* is an article° and a noun.° *I will be gone awhile* (not *a while*). *I will be gone for a while* (not *awhile*).

bad, badly   In formal speech and writing, *bad* should be used only as an adjective;° the adverb° is *badly. He felt bad because his tooth ached badly.* In *He felt bad,* the verb *felt* is a linking verb° and the adjective *bad* modifies the subject° *he,* not the verb *felt.*

being as, being that   Colloquial for *because,* the preferable word in formal speech or writing: *Because* (not *Being as*) *the world is round, Columbus never did fall off the edge.*

beside, besides   *Beside* is a preposition° meaning "next to." *Besides* is a preposition meaning "except" or "in addition to" as well as an adverb° meaning "in addition." *Besides, several other people besides you want to sit beside Dr. Christensen.*

between, among   See *among, between.*

bring, take   Use *bring* only for movement from a farther place to a nearer one and *take* for any other movement. *First, take these books to the library for renewal, then take them to Mr. Daniels. Bring them back to me when he's finished.*

can, may   Strictly, *can* indicates capacity or ability, and *may* indicates permission: *If I may talk with you a moment, I believe I can solve your problem.*

climatic, climactic   *Climatic* comes from *climate* and refers to weather: *Last winter's temperatures may indicate a climatic change. Climactic* comes from *climax* and refers to a dramatic high point: *During the climactic duel between Hamlet and Laertes, Gertrude drinks poisoned wine.*

complement, compliment   To *complement* something is to add to, complete, or reinforce it: *Her yellow blouse complemented her black hair.* To *compliment* something is to make a flattering remark about it: *He complimented her on her hair. Complimentary* can also mean "free": *complimentary tickets.*

conscience, conscious   *Conscience* is a noun° meaning "a sense of right and wrong"; *conscious* is an adjective° meaning "aware" or "awake." *Though I was barely conscious, my conscience nagged me.*

continual, continuous   *Continual* means "constantly recurring": *Most movies on television are continually interrupted by commercials. Continuous* means "unceasing": *Cable television often presents movies continuously without commercials.*

could of   See *have, of.*

criteria   The plural of *criterion* (meaning "standard for judgment"): *Of all our criteria for picking a roommate, the most important criterion is a sense of humor.*

data   The plural of *datum* (meaning "fact"). Though *data* is often used as a singular noun,° most careful writers still treat it as plural: *The data fail* (not *fails*) *to support the hypothesis.*

device, devise   *Device* is the noun,° and *devise* is the verb:° *Can you devise some device for getting his attention?*

different from, different than   *Different from* is preferred: *His purpose is different from mine.* But *different than* is widely accepted when a construction using *from* would be wordy: *I'm a different person now than I used to be* is preferable to *I'm a different person now from the person I used to be.*

disinterested, uninterested   *Disinterested* means "impartial": *We chose Pete, as a disinterested third party, to decide who was right. Uninterested* means "bored" or "lacking interest": *Unfortunately, Pete was completely uninterested in the question.*

don't   *Don't* is the contraction for *do not,* not for *does not: I don't care, you don't care,* but *he doesn't* (not *don't*) *care.*

due to   *Due* is always acceptable after a verb to refer back to the subject:° *His gray hairs were due to age.* Many object to *due to* meaning "because of" (*Due to the holiday, class was canceled*). A rule of thumb is that *due to* is always correct after a form of the verb *be* but questionable otherwise.

eager, anxious   See *anxious, eager.*

effect   See *affect, effect.*

elicit, illicit   *Elicit* is a verb° meaning "bring out" or "call forth." *Illicit* is an adjective° meaning "unlawful." *The crime elicited an outcry against illicit drugs.*

enthused   Used colloquially as an adjective° meaning "showing enthusiasm." The preferred adjective is *enthusiastic: The coach was enthusiastic* (not *enthused*) *about the team's victory.*

etc.   *Etc.,* the Latin abbreviation for "and other things," should be avoided in formal writing and should not be used to refer to people. When used, it should not substitute for precision, as in *The government provides health care, etc.,* and it should not end a list beginning *such as* or *for example.*

everybody, every body; everyone, every one   *Everybody* and *everyone* are indefinite pronouns:° *Everybody* (*everyone*) *knows Tom steals. Every one* is a pronoun° modified by *every,* and *every body* a noun° modified by *every.* Both refer to each thing or person of a specific group and are typically followed by *of: The game commissioner has stocked every body of fresh water in the state with fish, and now every one of our rivers is a potential trout stream.*

everyday, every day   *Everyday* is an adjective° meaning "used daily" or "common"; *every day* is a noun° modified by *every: Everyday problems tend to arise every day.*

everywheres   Nonstandard for *everywhere.*

except   See *accept, except.*

explicit, implicit   *Explicit* means "stated outright": *I left explicit instructions. Implicit* means "implied, unstated": *We had an implicit understanding.*

farther, further   *Farther* refers to additional distance (*How much farther is it to the beach?*), and *further* refers to additional time, amount, or other abstract matters (*I don't want to discuss this any further*).

fewer, less   *Fewer* refers to individual countable items (a plural noun°), *less* to general amounts (a singular noun): *Skim milk* *has fewer calories than whole milk. We have less milk left than I thought.*

further   See *farther, further.*

get   *Get* is easy to overuse; watch out for it in expressions such as *it's getting better* (substitute *improving*), *we got done* (substitute *finished*), and *the mayor has got to* (substitute *must*).

good, well   *Good* is an adjective,° and *well* is nearly always an adverb:° *Larry's a good dancer. He and Linda dance well together. Well* is properly used as an adjective only to refer to health: *You don't look well.* (*You look good,* in contrast, means "Your appearance is pleasing.")

hanged, hung   Though both are past-tense forms° of *hang, hanged* is used to refer to executions and *hung* is used for all other meanings: *Tom Dooley was hanged* (not *hung*) *from a white oak tree. I hung* (not *hanged*) *the picture you gave me.*

have, of   Use *have,* not *of,* after helping verbs° such as *could, should, would, may,* and *might: You should have* (not *should of*) *told me.*

he, she; he/she   Convention has allowed the use of *he* to mean "he or she," but most writers today consider this usage inaccurate and unfair because it excludes females. The construction *he/she,* one substitute for *he,* is awkward and objectionable to most readers. The better choice is to use *he or she,* to recast the sentence in the plural, or to rephrase. For instance: *After the infant learns to creep, he or she progresses to crawling. After infants learn to creep, they progress to crawling. After learning to creep, the infant progresses to crawling.* See also pp. 9–10 and 35.

herself, himself   See *myself, herself, himself, yourself.*

hisself   Nonstandard for *himself.*

hopefully   *Hopefully* means "with hope": *Freddy waited hopefully.* The use of *hopefully* to mean "it is to be hoped," "I hope," or "let's hope" is now very common; but since many readers continue to object strongly to the usage, you should avoid it. *I hope* (not *Hopefully*) *Eliza will be here soon.*

if, whether   For clarity, use *whether* rather than *if* when you are expressing an alternative: *If I laugh hard, people can't tell whether I'm crying.*

illicit   See *elicit, illicit.*

illusion   See *allusion, illusion.*

implicit   See *explicit, implicit.*

imply, infer   Writers or speakers *imply,* meaning "suggest": *Jim's letter implies he's having a good time.* Readers or listeners *infer,* meaning "conclude": *From Jim's letter I infer he's having a good time.*

irregardless   Nonstandard for *regardless.*

is, are   See *are, is.*

is when, is where   These are faulty constructions in sentences that define: *Adolescence is a stage* (not *is when a person is*) between *childhood and adulthood. Socialism is a system in which* (not *is where*) *government owns the means of production.*

its, it's   *Its* is the pronoun° *it* in the possessive case:° *That plant is losing its leaves. It's* is a contraction for *it is: It's likely to die if you don't water it.*

kind of, sort of, type of   In formal speech and writing, avoid using *kind of* or *sort of* to mean "somewhat": *He was rather* (not *kind of*) *tall.*

   Kind, sort, and *type* are singular: *This kind of dog is easily trained.* Errors often occur when these singular nouns are combined with the plural adjectives° *these* and *those: These kinds* (not *kind*) *of dogs are easily trained. Kind, sort,* and *type* should be followed by *of* but not by *a: I don't know what type of* (not *type* or *type of a*) *dog that is.*

   Use *kind of, sort of,* or *type of* only when the word *kind, sort,* or *type* is important: *That was a strange* (not *strange sort of*) *statement.*

lay, lie   *Lay* means "put" or "place" and takes a direct object:° *We could lay the tablecloth in the sun.* Its main forms are *lay, laid, laid. Lie* does not take an object and means "recline" or "be situated": *I lie awake at night. The town lies east of the river.* Its main forms are *lie, lay, lain.*

less   See *fewer, less.*

lie, lay   See *lay, lie.*

like, as   See *as, like.*

literally   This word means "actually" or "just as the words say," and it should not be used to intensify expressions whose words are not to be taken at face value. The sentence *He was literally climbing the walls* describes a person behaving like an insect, not a person who is restless or anxious. For the latter meaning, *literally* should be omitted.

lose, loose *Lose* means "mislay": *Did you lose a brown glove? Loose* usually means "unrestrained" or "not tight": *Ann's canary got loose.*

may, can See *can, may.*

may be, maybe *May be* is a verb,° and *maybe* is an adverb° meaning "perhaps": *Tuesday may be a legal holiday. Maybe we won't have classes.*

may of See *have, of.*

media *Media* is the plural of *medium* and takes a plural verb:° *All the news media are increasingly visual.*

might of See *have, of.*

must of See *have, of.*

myself, herself, himself, yourself The *-self* pronouns° refer to or intensify another word or words: *Paul and I did it ourselves; Jill herself said so.* In formal speech or writing, avoid using the *-self* pronouns in place of personal pronouns:° *No one except me* (not *myself*) *saw the accident.*

nowheres Nonstandard for *nowhere.*

number See *amount, number.*

of, have See *have, of.*

OK, O.K., okay All three spellings are acceptable, but avoid this colloquial term in formal speech and writing.

people, persons Except when emphasizing individuals, prefer *people* to *persons: We the people of the United States . . . ; Will the person or persons who saw the accident please notify. . . .*

percent (per cent), percentage Both these terms refer to fractions of one hundred. *Percent* always follows a numeral (*40 percent of the voters*), and the word should be used instead of the symbol (%) in general writing. *Percentage* usually follows an adjective (*a high percentage*).

persons See *people, persons.*

phenomena The plural of *phenomenon* (meaning "perceivable fact" or "unusual occurrence"): *The Center for Short-Lived Phenomena judged that the phenomenon we had witnessed was not a flying saucer.*

plus *Plus* is standard as a preposition° meaning "in addition to": *His income plus mine is sufficient.* But *plus* is colloquial as a conjunctive adverb:° *Our organization is larger than theirs; more-over* (not *plus*)*, we have more money.*

precede, proceed *Precede* means "come before": *My name pre-cedes yours in the alphabet. Proceed* means "move on": *We were told to proceed to the waiting room.*

prejudice, prejudiced *Prejudice* is a noun;° *prejudiced* is an ad-jective.° Do not drop the *-d* from *prejudiced: I was fortunate that my parents were not prejudiced* (not *prejudice*).

principal, principle *Principal* is an adjective° meaning "fore-most" or "major," a noun° meaning "chief official," or, in finance, a noun meaning "capital sum." *Principle* is a noun only, meaning "rule" or "axiom." *Her principal reasons for confessing were her principles of right and wrong.*

proceed, precede See *precede, proceed.*

raise, rise *Raise* means "lift" or "bring up" and takes a direct object:° *The Kirks raise cattle.* Its main forms are *raise, raised, raised. Rise* means "get up" and does not take an object: *They must rise at dawn.* Its main forms are *rise, rose, risen.*

real, really In formal speech and writing, *real* should not be used as an adverb;° *really* is the adverb and *real* an adjective.° *Popular reaction to the announcement was really* (not *real*) *enthu-siastic.*

reason is because Although colloquially common, this con-struction should be avoided in formal speech and writing. Use a *that* clause after *reason is: The reason he is absent is that* (not *is because*) *he is sick.* Or: *He is absent because he is sick.*

respectful, respective *Respectful* means "full of (or showing) respect": *Be respectful of other people. Respective* means "separate": *The French and the Germans occupied their respective trenches.*

rise, raise See *raise, rise.*

sensual, sensuous *Sensual* suggests sexuality; *sensuous* means "pleasing to the senses." *Stirred by the sensuous scent of meadow grass and flowers, Cheryl and Paul found their thoughts turning sensual.*

set, sit *Set* means "put" or "place" and takes a direct object:° *He sets the pitcher down.* Its main forms are *set, set, set. Sit* means "be seated" and does not take an object: *She sits on the sofa.* Its main forms are *sit, sat, sat.*

should of   See *have, of.*

since   *Since* mainly relates to time: *I've been waiting since noon.* But *since* is also often used to mean "because": *Since you ask, I'll tell you.* Revise sentences in which the word could mean either, such as *Since you left, my life is empty.*

sit, set   See *set, sit.*

somebody, some body; someone, some one   *Somebody* and someone are indefinite pronouns;° *some body* is a noun° modified by *some;* and *some one* is a pronoun° or an adjective° modified by *some. Somebody ought to invent a shampoo that will give hair some body. Someone told James he should choose some one plan and stick with it.*

sometime, sometimes, some time   *Sometime* means "at an indefinite time in the future": *Why don't you come up and see me sometime? Sometimes means "now and then": I still see my old friend Joe sometimes. Some time means "span of time": I need some time to make the payments.*

somewheres   Nonstandard for *somewhere.*

sort of, sort of a   See *kind of, sort of, type of.*

such as   See *like, such as.*

supposed to, used to   In both these expressions, the *-d* is essential: *I used to* (not *use to*) *think so. He's supposed to* (not *suppose to*) *meet us.*

sure and, sure to; try and, try to   *Sure to* and *try to* are the preferred forms: *Be sure to* (not *sure and*) *buy milk. Try to* (not *Try and*) *find some decent tomatoes.*

take, bring   See *bring, take.*

than, as   See *as, than.*

than, then   *Than* is a conjunction° used in comparisons, *then* an adverb° indicating time: *Holmes knew then that Moriarty was wilier than he had thought.*

that, which   *That* always introduces restrictive clauses:° *We should use the lettuce that Susan bought* (*that Susan bought* limits *lettuce* to a particular lettuce). *Which* can introduce both restrictive and nonrestrictive clauses,° but many writers reserve *which* only for nonrestrictive clauses: *The leftover lettuce, which is in the refrigerator, would make a good salad* (*which is in the refrigerator* simply provides more information about the lettuce).

their, there, they're   *Their* is the possessive° form of *they: Give them their money. There* indicates place (*I saw her standing there*) or functions as an expletive° (*There is a hole behind you*). *They're* is a contraction° for *they are: They're going fast.*

theirselves   Nonstandard for *themselves.*

then, than   See *than, then.*

these kind, these sort, these type, those kind   See *kind of, sort of, type of.*

thru   A colloquial spelling of *through* that should be avoided in all academic and business writing.

to, too, two   *To* is a preposition;° *too* is an adverb° meaning "also" or "excessively"; and *two* is a number. *I too have been to Europe two times.*

toward, towards   Both are acceptable, though *toward* is preferred. Use one or the other consistently.

try and, try to   See *sure and, sure to; try and, try to.*

type of   Don't use *type* without *of: It was a family type of* (not *type*) *restaurant.* Or, better: *It was a family restaurant.* See also *kind of, sort of, type of.*

uninterested   See *disinterested, uninterested.*

unique   *Unique* means "the only one of its kind" and so cannot sensibly by modified with words such as *very* or *most: That was a unique* (not *a very unique* or *the most unique*) *movie.*

used to   See *supposed to, used to.*

wait for, wait on   In formal speech and writing, *wait for* means "await" (*I'm waiting for Paul*), and *wait on* means "serve" (*The owner of the store herself waited on us*).

weather, whether   The *weather* is the state of the atmosphere. *Whether* introduces alternatives. *The weather will determine whether we go or not.*

well   See *good, well.*

whether, if   See *if, whether.*

which, who   *Which* never refers to people. Use *who* or sometimes *that* for a person or persons and *which* or *that* for a thing or things: *The baby, who was left behind, opened the door, which we had closed.*

who's, whose   *Who's* is the contraction° of *who is: Who's at the door? Whose* is the possessive° form of *who: Whose book is that?*

would have   Avoid this construction in place of *had* in clauses that begin *if* and state a condition contrary to fact: *If the tree had* (not *would have*) *withstood the fire, it would have been the oldest in town.*

would of   See *have, of.*

you   In all but very formal writing, *you* is generally appropriate as long as it means "you, the reader." In all writing, avoid indefinite uses of *you,* such as *In one ancient tribe your first loyalty was to your parents.*

your, you're   *Your* is the possessive° form of *you: Your dinner is ready. You're* is the contraction° of *you are: You're bound to be late.*

yourself   See *myself, herself, himself, yourself.*

GLOSSARY OF TERMS

This glossary defines the terms and concepts of basic English grammar, including every term marked ° in the text.

absolute phrase A phrase that consists of a noun° or pronoun° plus the *-ing* or *-ed* form of a verb° (a participle°): *Our accommodations arranged, we set out on our trip. They will hire a local person, other things being equal.*

active voice The verb form° used when the sentence subject° names the performer of the verb's action: *The drillers used a rotary blade.* For more, see *voice*.

adjective A word used to modify a noun° or pronoun:° *beautiful morning, ordinary one, good spelling.* Contrast *adverb*. Nouns and word groups may also serve as adjectives: *book sale; sale of old books; the sale, which occurs annually.*

adverb A word used to modify a verb,° an adjective,° another adverb, or a whole sentence: *warmly greet* (verb), *only three people* (adjective), *quite seriously* (adverb), *Fortunately, she is employed* (sentence). Word groups may also serve as adverbs: *drove by a farm, plowed the fields when the earth thawed.*

agreement The correspondence of one word to another in person,° number,° or gender.° Mainly, a verb° must agree with its subject° (*The chef orders eggs*), and a pronoun° must agree with it antecedent° (*The chef surveys her breakfast*). See also pp. 25–27.

antecedent The word a pronoun° refers to: *Jonah, who is not yet ten, has already chosen the college he will attend* (*Jonah* is the antecedent of the pronouns *who* and *he*).

appositive A word or word group appearing next to a noun° or pronoun° that explains or identifies it and is equivalent to it: *My brother Michael, the best horn player in town, won the state competition* (*Michael* identifies which brother is being referred to; *the best horn player in town* adds information about *My brother Michael*).

article The words *a, an,* and *the.* Articles always signal that a noun follows. See p. 114 for how to choose between *a* and *an.* See pp. 40–41 for the rules governing *a/an* and *the.*

126

auxiliary verb   See *helping verb.*

case   The form of a pronoun° or noun° that indicates its function in the sentence. Most pronouns have three cases. The SUBJECTIVE CASE is for subjects° and subject complements:° *I, you, he, she, it, we, they, who, whoever.* The OBJECTIVE CASE is for objects:° *me, you, him, her, it, us, them, whom, whomever.* The POSSESSIVE CASE is for ownership: *my/mine, your/yours, his, her/hers, its, our/ours, their/theirs, whose.* Nouns take the subjective case (*dog, America*) for all cases except the possessive (*dog's, America's*).

clause   A group of words containing a subject° and a predicate.° A MAIN CLAUSE can stand alone as a sentence: <u>We can go to the movies</u>. A SUBORDINATE CLAUSE cannot stand alone as a sentence: *We can go <u>if Julie gets back on time</u>*. For more, see *subordinate clause.*

collective noun   A word with singular form that names a group of individuals or things: for instance, *team, army, family, flock, group.*

comma splice   A sentence error in which two sentences (main clauses°) are separated by a comma without *and, but, or, nor,* or another coordinating conjunction.° Splice: *The book was long, it contained useful information.* Revised: *The book was long; it contained useful information.* Or: *The book was long, <u>and</u> it contained useful information.* See pp. 46–48.

comparison   The form of an adverb° or adjective° that shows its degree of quality or amount. The POSITIVE is the simple, uncompared form: *gross, clumsily.* The COMPARATIVE compares the thing modified to at least one other thing: *grosser, more clumsily.* The SUPERLATIVE indicates that the thing modified exceeds all other things to which it is being compared: *grossest, most clumsily.* The comparative and superlative are formed either with the endings *-er* and *-est* or with the words *more* and *most* or *less* and *least.*

complement   See *subject complement.*

complex sentence   See *sentence.*

compound-complex sentence   See *sentence.*

compound construction   Two or more words or word groups serving the same function, such as a compond subject° (*<u>Harriet and Peter</u> poled their barge down the river*), a compound predicate° (*The scout <u>watched and waited</u>*), or a compound sentence (*<u>He smiled, and I laughed</u>*).

---

128 · Glossary of terms

compound sentence   See *sentence.*

conditional statement   A statement expressing a condition contrary to fact and using the subjunctive mood° of the verb: *If she were mayor, the unions would cooperate.*

conjunction   A word that links and relates parts of a sentence. See *coordinating conjunction* (*and, but,* etc.), *correlative conjunction* (*either . . . or, both . . . and,* etc.), and *subordinating conjunction* (*because, if,* etc.).

conjunctive adverb   An adverb° that relates two complete sentences (main clauses°) in a single sentence: *We had hoped to own a house by now; however, prices are still too high.* The main clauses are separated by a semicolon. Some common conjunctive adverbs: *accordingly, also, anyway, besides, certainly, consequently, finally, further, furthermore, hence, however, incidentally, indeed, instead, likewise, meanwhile, moreover, namely, nevertheless, next, nonetheless, now, otherwise, similarly, still, then, thereafter, therefore, thus, undoubtedly.*

contraction   A condensed expression, with an apostrophe replacing the missing letters: for example, *doesn't* (*does not*), *we'll* (*we will*).

coordinating conjunction   A word linking words or word groups serving the same function: *The dog and cat sometimes fight, but they usually get along.* The coordinating conjunctions are *and, but, or, nor, for, so, yet.*

coordination   The linking of words or word groups that are of equal importance, usually with a coordinating conjunction.° *He and I laughed, but she was not amused.* Contrast *subordination.*

correlative conjunction   Two or more connecting words that work together to link words or word groups serving the same function: *Both Michiko and June signed up, but neither Stan nor Carlos did.* The correlatives include *both . . . and, not only . . . but also, not . . . but, either . . . or, neither . . . nor, whether . . . or, as . . . as.*

count noun   A word that names a person, place, or thing that can be counted (and so may appear in plural form): *camera/cameras, river/rivers, child/children.*

dangling modifier   A modifier that does not sensibly modify anything in its sentence. Dangling: *Having arrived late, the concert had already begun.* Revised: *Having arrived late, we found that the concert had already begun.* See p. 43.

determiner A word such as *a, an, the, my,* and *your* that indicates that a noun follows. See also *article.*

direct address A construction in which a word or phrase indicates the person or group spoken to: *Have you finished, John? Farmers, unite.*

direct object A noun° or pronoun° that identifies who or what receives the action of a verb:° *Education opens doors.* For more, see *object* and *predicate.*

direct question A sentence asking a question and concluding with a question mark: *Do they know we are watching?* Contrast *indirect question.*

double negative A nonstandard form consisting of two negative words used in the same construction so that they effectively cancel each other: *I don't have no money.* Rephrase as *I have no money* or *I don't have any money.*

ellipsis The omission of a word or words from a quotation, indicated by the three spaced periods of an ELLIPSIS MARK: *"that all . . . are created equal."*

expletive construction A sentence that postpones the subject° by beginning with *there* or *it* and a form of *be: It is impossible to get a ticket. There are no more seats available.*

first person See *person.*

fused sentence (run-on sentence) A sentence error in which two complete sentences (main clauses°) are joined with no punctuation or connecting word between them. Fused: *I heard his lecture it was dull.* Revised: *I heard his lecture; it was dull.* See pp. 46–48.

future perfect tense The verb tense expressing an action that will be completed before another future action: *They will have heard by then.* For more, see *tense.*

future tense The verb tense expressing action that will occur in the future: *They will hear soon.* For more, see *tense.*

gender The classification of nouns° or pronouns° as masculine (*he, boy*), feminine (*she, woman*), or neuter (*it, typewriter*).

gerund A verb form that ends in *-ing* and functions as a noun:° *Working is all right for killing time.* For more, see *verbals and verbal phrases.*

gerund phrase See *verbals and verbal phrases*

TERMS

helping verb (auxiliary verb) A verb° used with another verb to convey time, possibility, obligation, and other meanings: *You should write a letter. You have written other letters.* The MODALS are the following: *can, could, may, might, must, ought, shall, should, will, would.* The other helping verbs are forms of *be, have,* and *do.*

idiom An expression that is peculiar to a language and that may not make sense if taken literally: for example, *dark horse, bide your time,* and *by and large.*

imperative See *mood.*

indefinite pronoun A word that stands for a noun° and does not refer to a specific person or thing: *all, any, anybody, anyone, anything, each, either, everybody, everyone, everything, neither, nobody, none, no one, nothing, one, some, somebody, someone, something.* Indefinite pronouns usually take singular verbs and are referred to by singular pronouns (*something makes its presence* felt). See also pp. 26, 34–35.

indicative See *mood.*

indirect object A noun° or pronoun° that identifies to whom or what something is done: *Give them the award.* For more, see *object* and *predicate.*

indirect question A sentence reporting a question and ending with a period: *Writers wonder if their work must always be lonely.* Contrast *direct question.*

infinitive A verb form° consisting of the verb's dictionary form plus *to: to swim, to write.* For more, see *verbals and verbal phrases.*

infinitive phrase See *verbals and verbal phrases.*

intensive pronoun See *pronoun.*

interjection A word standing by itself or inserted in a construction to exclaim or command attention: *Hey! Ouch! What the heck did you do that for?*

interrogative pronoun See *pronoun.*

intransitive verb A verb° that does not require a following word (direct object°) to complete its meaning: *Mosquitoes buzz. The hospital may close.* For more, see *predicate.*

irregular verb See *verb forms.*

linking verb A verb that links, or connects, a subject° and a word that renames or describes the subject (a subject complement°): *They are golfers. You seem lucky.* The linking verbs are the forms of *be*, the verbs of the senses (*look, sound, smell, feel, taste*), and a few others (*appear, become, grow, prove, remain, seem, turn*). For more, see *predicate*.

main clause   A word group that contains a subject° and a predicate,° does not begin with a subordinating word, and may stand alone as a sentence: *The president was not overbearing.* For more, see *clause*.

main verb   The part of a verb phrase° that carries the principal meaning: *had been <u>walking</u>, could <u>happen</u>, was <u>chilled</u>.* Contrast *helping verb*.

mass noun   A word that names a person, place, or thing and that is not considered countable in English (and so does not appear in plural form): *confidence, information, silver, work.*

misplaced modifier   A modifier so far from the term it modifies or so close to another term it could modify that its relation to the rest of the sentence is unclear. Misplaced: *The children played with firecrackers that they bought illegally <u>in the field</u>.* Revised: *The children played <u>in the field</u> with firecrackers that they bought illegally.*

modal   See *helping verb*.

modifier   Any word or word group that limits or qualifies the meaning of another word or word group. Modifiers include adjectives° and adverbs° as well as words and word groups that act as adjectives and adverbs.

mood   The form of a verb° that shows how the speaker views the action. The INDICATIVE MOOD, the most common, is used to make statements or ask questions: *The play <u>will be performed</u> Saturday. <u>Did</u> you <u>get</u> tickets?* The IMPERATIVE MOOD gives a command: *Please <u>get</u> good seats. <u>Avoid</u> the top balcony.* The SUBJUNCTIVE MOOD expresses a wish, a condition contrary to fact, a recommendation, or a request: *I wish George <u>were coming</u> with us. If he <u>were</u> here, he'd come.*

nonrestrictive clause   See *nonrestrictive element*.

nonrestrictive element   A word or word group that does not limit the word it refers to and that is not essential to the meaning of the sentence. Nonrestrictive elements are usually set off by commas: *Sleep, <u>which we all need,</u> occupies a third of our lives. His wife, <u>Patricia,</u> is a chemist.* Contrast *restrictive element*.

noun   A word that names a person, place, thing, quality, or idea: *Maggie, Alabama, clarinet, satisfaction, socialism.* See also *collective noun, count noun, mass noun, proper noun*.

noun clause See *clause.*

number The form of a word that indicates whether it is singular or plural. Singular: *I, he, this, child, runs, hides.* Plural: *we, they, these, children, run, hide.*

object A noun° or pronoun° that receives the action of or is influenced by another word. A DIRECT OBJECT receives the action of a verb° or verbal° and usually follows it in a sentence: *We watched the stars.* An INDIRECT OBJECT tells for or to whom something is done: *Reiner bought us tapes.* An OBJECT OF A PREPOSITION usually follows a preposition° and is linked by it to the rest of the sentence: *They are going to New Orleans for the jazz festival.*

objective case The form of a pronoun° when it is the object° of a verb° (*call him*) or the object of a preposition° (*for us*). For more, see *case.*

object of preposition See *object.*

parallelism Similarity of grammatical form between two or more coordinated elements: *Rising prices and declining incomes left many people in bad debt and worse despair.* See pp. 4–5.

parenthetical element A word or construction that interrupts a sentence and is not part of its main structure, called *parenthetical* because it could (or does) appear in parentheses: *Mary Cassatt (1845–1926) was an American painter. Her work, incidentally, is in the museum.*

participial phrase See *verbals and verbal phrases.*

participle See *verbals and verbals phrases.*

particle A preposition° or adverb° in a two-word verb: *catch on, look up.*

parts of speech The classes into which words are commonly grouped according to their form, function, and meaning: nouns, pronouns, verbs, adjectives, adverbs, conjunctions, prepositions, and interjections. See separate entries for each part of speech.

passive voice The verb form° used when the sentence subject° names the receiver of the verb's action: *The mixture was stirred.* For more, see *voice.*

past participle The *-ed* form of most verbs:° *fished, hopped.* Some verbs form their past participles in irregular ways: *begun, written.* For more, see *verbals and verbal phrases* and *verb forms.*

past perfect tense   The verb tense expressing an action that was completed before another past action: *No one had heard that before.* For more, see *tense.*

past tense   The verb tense expressing action that occurred in the past: *Everyone laughed.* For more, see *tense.*

past-tense form   The verb form used to indicate action that occurred in the past, usually created by adding *-d* or *-ed* to the verb's dictionary form (*smiled*) but created differently for most irregular verbs (*began, threw*). For more, see *verb forms.*

perfect tenses   The verb tenses indicating action completed before another specific time or action: *have walked, had walked, will have walked.* For more, see *tense.*

person   The form of a verb° or pronoun° that indicates whether the subject is speaking, spoken to, or spoken about. In the FIRST PERSON the subject is speaking: *I am, we are.* In the SECOND PERSON the subject is spoken to: *you are.* In the THIRD PERSON the subject is spoken about: *he/she/it is, they are.*

personal pronoun   *I, you, he, she, it, we,* or *they:* a word that substitutes for a specific noun° or other pronoun. For more, see *case.*

phrase   A group of related words that lacks a subject° or a predicate° or both: *She ran into the field. She tried to jump the fence.* See also *absolute phrase, prepositional phrase, verbals and verbal phrases.*

plain form   The dictionary form of a verb: *make, run, swivel.* For more, see *verb forms.*

plural   More than one. See *number.*

positive form   See *comparison.*

possessive case   The form of a noun° or pronoun° that indicates its ownership of something else: *men's attire, your briefcase.* For more, see *case.*

predicate   The part of a sentence that makes an assertion about the subject.° The predicate may consist of an intransitive verb° (*The earth trembled*), a transitive verb° plus a direct object° (*The earthquake shook buildings*), a linking verb° plus subject complement° (*The result was chaos*), a transitive verb plus indirect object° and direct object (*The government sent the city aid*), or a transitive verb plus direct object and object complement (*the citizens considered the earthquake a disaster*).

preposition A word that forms a noun° or pronoun° (plus any modifiers) into a PREPOSITIONAL PHRASE: *about* love, *down* the steep stairs. The common prepositions: *about, above, according to, across, after, against, along, along with, among, around, as, at, because of, before, behind, below, beneath, beside, between, beyond, by, concerning, despite, during, except, except for, excepting, for, from, in, in addition to, inside, in spite of, instead of, into, like, near, next to, of, off, on, onto, out, out of, outside, over, past, regarding, since, through, throughout, till, to, toward, under, underneath, unlike, until, up, upon, with, within, without.*

prepositional phrase A word group consisting of a preposition° and its object.° Prepositional phrases usually serve as adjectives° (*We saw a movie about sorrow*) and as adverbs° (*We went back for the second show*).

present participle The *-ing* form of a verb:° *swimming, flying.* For more, see *verbals and verbal phrases.*

present perfect tense The verb tense expressing action that began in the past and is linked to the present: *Dogs have buried bones here before.* For more, see *tense.*

present tense The verb tense expressing action that is occurring now, occurs habitually, or is generally true: *Dogs bury bones here often.* For more, see *tense.*

principal parts The three forms of a verb from which its various tenses are created: the PLAIN FORM (*stop, go*), the PAST-TENSE FORM (*stopped, went*), and the PAST PARTICIPLE (*stopped, gone*). For more, see *tense* and *verb forms.*

progressive tenses The verb tenses that indicate continuing (progressive) action and use the *-ing* form of the verb: *A dog was burying a bone here this morning.* For more, see *tense.*

pronoun A word used in place of a noun,° such as *I, he, everyone, who,* and *herself.* See also *indefinite pronoun, personal pronoun, relative pronoun.*

proper noun A word naming a specific person, place, or thing and beginning with a capital letter: *Arsenio Hall, Mt. Rainier, Washington, U.S. Congress.*

regular verb See *verb forms.*

relative pronoun *Who, whoever, which,* or *that:* a word that relates a group of words to a noun° or other pronoun:° *Ask the woman who knows all. This may be the question that stumps her.* For more, see *case.*

restrictive clause See *restrictive element.*

restrictive element   A word or word group that is essential to the meaning of the sentence because it limits the word it refers to: removing it would leave the meaning unclear or too general. Restrictive elements are *not* set off by commas: *Dorothy's companion the Scarecrow lacks a brain. The man who called about the apartment said he'd try again.* Contrast *nonrestrictive element.*

run-on sentence   See *fused sentence.*

-s form   See *verb forms.*

second person   See *person.*

sentence   A complete unit of thought, consisting of at least a subject° and a predicate° that are not introduced by a subordinating word. Sentences can be classed on the basis of their structure: A SIMPLE SENTENCE contains one main clause:° *I'm leaving.* A COMPOUND SENTENCE contains at least two main clauses: *I'd like to stay, but I'm leaving.* A COMPLEX SENTENCE contains one main clause and at least one subordinate clause:° *If you let me go now, you'll be sorry.* A COMPOUND-COMPLEX SENTENCE contains at least two main clauses and at least one subordinate clause: *I'm leaving because you want me to, but I'd rather stay.*

sentence fragment   A sentence error in which a group of words is set off as a sentence even though it begins with a subordinating word or lacks a subject° or a predicate° or both. Fragment: *She was not in shape for the race. Which she had hoped to win.* Revised: *She was not in shape for the race, which she had hoped to win.* See pp. 45–46.

series   Three or more items with the same function: *We gorged on ham, eggs, and potatoes.*

simple sentence   See *sentence.*

simple tenses   See *tense.*

singular   One. See *number.*

split infinitive   The usually awkward interruption of an infinitive° and its marker *to* by a modifier: *Management decided to not introduce the new product.* See p. 43.

squinting modifier   A modifier that could modify the words on either side of it: *The plan we considered seriously worries me.*

subject   In grammar, the part of a sentence that names something and about which an assertion is made in the predicate:° *The quick, brown fox jumped lazily* (simple subject); *The quick, brown fox jumped lazily* (complete subject).

subject complement   A word that renames or describes the subject° of a sentence, after a linking verb:° *The stranger was a man* (noun°). *He seemed gigantic* (adjective°).

subjective case   The form of a pronoun° when it is the subject° of a sentence (*I called*) or a subject complement° (*It was I*). For more, see *case.*

subjunctive   See *mood.*

subordinate clause   A word group that consists of a subject° and a predicate,° begins with a subordinating word such as *because* or *who,* and is not a question: *They voted for whoever seemed to care the least because they mistrusted politicians.* Subordinate clauses may serve as adjectives° (*The car that hit Fred was running a red light*), as adverbs° (*The car hit Fred when it ran a red light*), or as nouns° (*Whoever was driving should be arrested*). Subordinate clauses may *not* serve as complete sentences.

subordinating conjunction   A word that forms a complete sentence into a word group (a subordinate clause°) that can serve as an adverb° or a noun.° *Everyone was relieved when the meeting ended.* Some common subordinating conjunctions: *after, although, as, as if, as long as, as though, because, before, even if, even though, if, if only, in order that, now that, once, rather than, since, so that, than, that, though, till, unless, until, when, whenever, where, whereas, wherever, while.*

subordination   The use of grammatical structures to deemphasize one element in a sentence by making it dependent on rather than equal to another. Through subordination, *I left six messages; the doctor failed to call* becomes *Although I left six messages, the doctor failed to call* or *After six messages, the doctor failed to call.*

tag question   A question attached to the end of a statement and composed of a pronoun,° a helping verb,° and sometimes the word *not: It isn't raining, is it? It is sunny, isn't it?*

tense   The form of a verb° that expresses the time of its action, usually indicated by the verb's endings and by helping verbs. See also *verb forms.*

PRESENT: action that is occurring now, occurs habitually, or is generally true

SIMPLE PRESENT: plain form or *-s* form	PRESENT PROGRESSIVE: *am, is,* or *are* plus *-ing* form
I *walk.*	I *am walking.*
You/we/they *walk.*	You/we/they *are walking.*
He/she/it *walks.*	He/she/it *is walking.*

PAST: action that occurred before now

SIMPLE PAST: past-tense form (*-d* or *-ed*)	PAST PROGRESSIVE: *was* or *were* plus *-ing* form
I/he/she/it *walked*. You/we/they *walked*.	I/he/she/it *was walking*. You/we/they *were walking*.

FUTURE: action that will occur in the future

SIMPLE FUTURE: plain form plus *will*	FUTURE PROGRESSIVE: *will be* plus *-ing* form
I/you/he/she/it/we/they *will walk*.	I/you/he/she/it/we/they *will be walking*.

PRESENT PERFECT: action that began in the past and is linked to the present

PRESENT PERFECT: *have* or *has* plus past participle (*-d* or *-ed*)	PRESENT PERFECT PROGRESSIVE: *have been* or *has been* plus *-ing* form
I/you/we/they *have walked*.	I/you/we/they *have been walking*.
He/she/it *has walked*.	He/she/it *has been walking*.

PAST PERFECT: action that was completed before another past action

PAST PERFECT: *had* plus past participle (*-d* or *-ed*)	PAST PERFECT PROGRESSIVE: *had been* plus *-ing* form
I/you/he/she/it/we/they *had walked*.	I/you/he/she/it/we/they *had been walking*.

FUTURE PERFECT: action that will be completed before another future action

FUTURE PERFECT: *will have* plus past participle (*-d* or *-ed*)	FUTURE PERFECT PROGRESSIVE: *will have been* plus *-ing* form
I/you/he/she/it/we/they *will have walked*.	I/you/he/she/it/we/they *will have been walking*.

transitive verb   A verb° that requires a following word (a direct object°) to complete its meaning: *We raised the roof.* For more, see *predicate*.

verb   A word that expresses an action (*bring, change*), an occurrence (*happen, become*), or a state of being (*be, seem*). A verb is the essential word in a predicate,° the part of a sentence that makes an assertion about the subject.° With endings and helping verbs,° verbs can indicate tense,° mood,° voice,° number,° and person.° For more, see separate entries for each of these aspects as well as *verb forms*.

TERMS

verbals and verbal phrases   VERBALS are verb forms used as adjectives,° adverbs,° or nouns.° They form VERBAL PHRASES with objects° and modifiers. A PRESENT PARTICIPLE adds *-ing* to the dictionary form of a verb (*living*). A PAST PARTICIPLE usually adds *-d* or *-ed* to the dictionary form (*lived*), although irregular verbs form the past participle in other ways (*begun, swept*). A participle or PARTICIPIAL PHRASE usually serves as an adjective: *Strolling shop-* *pers fill the malls.* A GERUND is the *-ing* form of a verb used as a noun. Gerunds and GERUND PHRASES can do whatever nouns can do: *Shopping satisfies personal needs.* An INFINITIVE is the verb's dictionary form plus *to: to live.* Infinitives and INFINITIVE PHRASES may serve as nouns (*To design a mall is to create an artificial environment*), as adverbs (*Malls are designed to make shoppers feel safe*), or as adjectives (*The environment supports the impulse to shop*).

Note that a verbal *cannot* serve as the only verb in the predicate° of a sentence. For that, it requires a helping verb:° *Shoppers were strolling.*

verb forms   Verbs have five distinctive forms. The PLAIN FORM is the dictionary form: *A few artists live in town today.* The -S FORM adds *-s* or *-es* to the plain form: *The artist lives in town today.* The PAST-TENSE FORM usually adds *-d* or *-ed* to the plain form: *Many artists lived in town before this year.* Some verbs' past-tense forms are irregular, such as *began, fell, swam, threw, wrote.* The PAST PARTICIPLE is usually the same as the past-tense form, although, again, some verbs' past participles are irregular (*begun, fallen, swum, thrown, written*). The PRESENT PARTICIPLE adds *-ing* to the plain form: *A few artists are living in town today.*

REGULAR VERBS are those that add *-d* or *-ed* to the plain form for the past-tense form and past participle. IRREGULAR VERBS create these forms in irregular ways (see above).

verb phrase   See *phrase.* A verb° of more than one word that serves as the predicate° of a sentence: The movie *has started.*

voice   The form of a verb° that tells whether the sentence subject° performs the action or is acted upon. In the ACTIVE VOICE the subject acts: *The city controls rents.* In the PASSIVE VOICE the subject is acted upon: *Rents are controlled by the city.* The actor in a passive sentence may be stated (*the city*) or not stated: *Rents are controlled.*

INDEX

a, an, 126
  capitalization in titles, 73
  choosing between, 114
  rules for use of (ESL), 40–41
Abbreviations
  a vs. *an* with, 114
  acceptable, 76
  B.C., A.D., A.M., P.M., no., $,
    76
  for calendar designations, 77
  for courses of instruction, 77
  for frequently used terms, 76
  for geographical names, 77
  Latin, 76–77
  for names of people, 77
  period in, 50, 76
  with specific dates and num-
    bers, 76
  for titles with names, 75
  for units of measurement, 77
Absolute phrases, 52, 126
Abstract, dissertation
  MLA style for, 97
  note for, 111
Abstract words, 11–12
accept, except, 114
Acknowledgment of sources
  necessity for, 84
  using APA style, 100–07
  using MLA style, 87–100
  using notes, 107–13
Active voice
  consistency in use of, 24
  definition of, 24, 126
  vs. passive voice, 14, 24–25,
    126
A.D., B.C., 76
Address (lecture)
  MLA style for, 99
  underlining (italics) for, 74
Addresses (street, city, state),
    53, 78
Adjectives
  vs. adverbs, 38
  comma with two or more, 53
  comparative and superlative
    forms of, 38–39
  definition of, 38, 126
  hyphen in compound, 71
  irregular, 39

after linking verbs, 38
to modify nouns and pro-
  nouns, 38, 126
order of (ESL), 43
present vs. past participles
  as (ESL), 40
proper, capitalization of, 72–
  73
Adverbs. *See also* Conjunctive
  adverbs
  vs. adjectives, 138, 126
  comparative and superlative
    forms of, 38–39
  definition of, 38, 126
  irregular, 39
  to modify verbs, adjectives,
    adverbs, 38
  semicolon with main clauses
    related by, 48
  in two-word verbs (ESL),
    29–30
advice, advise, 114
affect, effect, 114
Afterword of book, MLA style
  for, 96
Agreement of pronouns and
  antecedents, 33–35
  with antecedents joined by
    and, 34
  with antecedents joined by
    or or *nor,* 34
  definition of, 126
  with *everyone* and other in-
    definite pronouns, 34–35
  with *team* and other collec-
    tive nouns, 35
Agreement of subjects and
  verbs, 25–27
  definition of, 126
  with *everyone* and other in-
    definite pronouns, 26
  with intervening words, 25
  with inverted word order, 27
  with linking verbs, 27
  with singular words ending
    in -*s,* 27
  with subjects joined by *and,*
    25–26
  with subjects joined by *or* or
    nor, 26

139

144 · Index

146 · Index

INDEX

EDITING SYMBOLS

Your readers may use some of these symbols to mark editing you should do. Page numbers refer you to relevant sections of this handbook.

ab	Faulty abbreviation 75	. ? !	Period, question mark, exclamation point 50
ad	Misuse of adjective or adverb 38	⌃	Comma 51
agr	Error in agreement 25, 33	;	Semicolon 54
		:	Colon 56
ap	Apostrophe needed or misused 57	⌄	Apostrophe 57
appr	Inappropriate word 7	" "	Quotation marks 59
awk	Awkward construction	— ( ) … [ ] /	Dash, parentheses, ellipsis mark, brackets, slash 61
case	Error in pronoun case 31		
cap	Use capital letter 72	par, ¶	Start new paragraph
cit	Missing source citation or error in form of citation 87–113	pass	Ineffective passive voice 14, 24
con	Be more concise 12	pn agr	Error in pronoun-antecedent agreement 33
coord	Coordination needed 2	ref	Error in pronoun reference 35
cs	Comma splice 46		
d	Ineffective diction (word choice) 7–12	rep	Unnecessary repetition 13
det	Add details 7	shift	Inconsistency 21, 23, 24, 37
dm	Dangling modifier 43		
emph	Emphasis lacking 3	sp	Misspelled word
exact	Inexact word 10	spec	Be more specific 7, 11
frag	Sentence fragment 45	sub	Subordination needed 3
fs	Fused sentence 46	t	Error in verb tense 20
gl/us	See Glossary of Usage 114	t seq	Error in tense sequence 21
hyph	Error in use of hyphen 71	trans	Transition needed
		und	Underline (italicize) 74
inc	Incomplete construction	var	Vary sentence structure 5
ital	Italicize (underline) 74		
k	Awkward construction	vb	Error in verb form 17
lc	Use lowercase letter 72	vb agr	Error in subject-verb agreement 25
mm	Misplaced modifier 42		
mng	Meaning unclear	w	Wordy 12
ms	Error in manuscript form 27	ww	Wrong word 10
		/ /	Faulty parallelism 4
no cap	Unnecessary capital letter 72	#	Separate with a space
no ⌃	Comma not needed 51	⌢	Close up space
no ¶	No new paragraph needed	⬝	Delete
num	Error in use of numbers 77	teh	Transpose letters or words
		x	Obvious error
p	Error in punctuation 50–63	⌃	Something missing
		??	Manuscript illegible or meaning unclear